Baedeker's TOKYO

Imprint

Cover picture: Imperial Palace

77 colour photographs
7 plans, 1 subways map, 1 large city map

Conception and editorial work:
Redaktionsbüro Harenberg, Schwerte

English language: Alec Court

Text:
Hans Kirchmann

General direction:
Dr Peter Baumgarten, Baedeker Stuttgart

English translation: C. N. Smith (Babel Translations Norwich)

Cartography:
Ingenieurbüro für Kartographie Huber & Oberländer, Munich
Shobunsha Co., Ltd, Tokyo (city map)

Source of illustrations:
dpa (35), Japan National Tourist Organisation (21), Kirchmann (12), Messerschmidt (8),
Sperber (1)

Following the tradition established by Karl Baedeker in 1844, sights of particular interest and hotels of outstanding quality are distinguished by either one or two asterisks.

To make it easier to locate the various sights listed in the "A to Z" section of the Guide, their coordinates on the large map of Tokyo are shown in red at the head of each entry.

Only a selection of hotels, shops and restaurants can be given: no reflection is implied, therefore, on establishments not included.

In a time of rapid change it is difficult to ensure that all the information given is entirely accurate and up to date, and the possibility of error can never be entirely eliminated. Although the publishers can accept no responsibility for inaccuracies and omissions they are always grateful for corrections and suggestions for improvement.

© Baedeker Stuttgart
Original German edition

© 1987 Jarrold and Sons Ltd
English language edition worldwide

© 1987 The Automobile Association 57037
United Kingdom and Ireland

US and Canadian edition
Prentice Hall Press

Licensed user:
Mairs Geographischer Verlag GmbH & Co., Ostfildern-Kemnat bei Stuttgart

Reproductions:
Gölz Repro-Service GmbH, Ludwigsburg

The name *Baedeker* is a registered trademark

Printed in Great Britain by Jarrold & Sons Ltd Norwich

0-13-058108-9

Contents

Preface

This Pocket Guide to Tokyo is one of the new generation of Baedeker city guides.

Baedeker pocket guides, illustrated throughout in colour, are designed to meet the needs of the modern traveller. They are quick and easy to consult, with the principal sights described in alphabetical order and practical details about opening times, how to get there, etc., shown in the margin.

Each guide is divided into three parts. The first part gives a general account of the city, its history, population, culture and so on; in the second part the principal sights are described; and the third part contains a variety of practical information designed to help visitors to find their way about and make the most of their stay.

The new guides are abundantly illustrated and contain numbers of newly drawn plans. At the back of the book is a large city map, and each entry in the main part of the guide gives the coordinates of the square on the map in which the particular feature can be located. Users of this guide, therefore will have no difficulty in finding what they want to see.

Facts and Figures

Tokyo

General

In Japanese this East Asian state is called Nippon, that is to say "Land of the Rising Sun". Its area is 145,737 sq. miles (377,458 sq. km) and comprises four main islands – Honshu, Hokkaido, Kyushu and Shikoku – and some 3500 smaller islands.	The State

Many regional dialects are spoken in Japan. The language spoken in the city of Tokyo, however, has established itself as the standard language of social and commercial intercourse.

The Japanese language possesses a wide range of modes of expression. The form of expression employed is affected by age and sex and also by the requirements of courtesy and modesty. The basic vocabulary of the Japanese language is bi-syllabic for the most part. Compound formulations are, however, very common.

Foreign linguistic borrowings came in earlier times from Portuguese and Dutch, and specialised medical and philosophical terminology was derived from German. Nowadays American is virtually the sole source of new words.

Language

Japanese script was derived about A.D. 400 from the Chinese script which has only ideograms for monosyllabic words and no abstract characters for sounds and syllables. Syllable characters were derived from the Chinese characters in the course of time, because the Japanese language, which is polysyllabic in nature, cannot manage without them. Ideograms were, however, also adopted, and in such cases the written form gives no hint about the pronunciation of the word. Japanese script is, therefore, a mixture employing some 50 phonetic characters and about 8000 ideograms (Kanji). Elementary schoolchildren are expected to learn about 1500 Kanji. Traditional writing runs in vertical files from right to left. Transliteration into the Roman alphabet is difficult; the Hepburn system, so-called after the American missionary C. Hepburn, is the one most commonly used.

Script

Tokyo is the capital city of the parliamentary democratic monarchy of Japan, the Imperial Residence with the Emperor's Palace, and the seat of Government and of Parliament.

Capital

Tokyo is situated in E Central-Honshu, the largest of Japan's main islands.

Region

Tokyo's latitude is 35°N, its longitude 140°E. The city lies N of The Bay of Tokyo, between the River Arakawa to the E and the River Tama to the W.

Geographical position

International Telephone Codes
The prefix for telephone calls
from the United Kingdom is 010 81

Dialling code

◄ *View of Tokyo and out over the city*

from the United States or Canada is 011 81
Calls from Japan to Europe are put through by Kokusai Denshin
Denwa Co. Ltd (KDD), Tokyo; tel. (03) 211 5111
For international calls from Tokyo and Osaka dial 00 51
For calls from Tokyo to Europe dial 0051 ("KDD" means
Central Telephone Exchange). Outside Tokyo the number is
03–2115511.

Area and population

When speaking of Tokyo it is essential to distinguish between
the Prefecture of Tokyo and the more circumscribed concept of
Tokyo City.
The Prefecture, the metropolitan district of Tokyo, comprises
23 districts (or "ku"), 26 cities, 7 urban districts and 8 villages.
Two urban districts and 7 villages lie on the islands of Izu and
Ogasawara which come under Tokyo for administrative
purposes. The Prefecture covers an area of 831 sq. miles (2410
sq. km). Its population is approximately 12,000,000.

"Ku" (districts)

The names of the districts are: Chiyoda, Bunkyo, Meguro,
Taito, Adachi, Nerima, Ota, Itabashi, Chuo, Toshima, Sumida,
Katushika, Nakano, Shinagawa, Kita, Koto, Edogawa, Sugi-
nami, Arakawa, Shibuya, Setagaya, Minato and Shinjuku.
Tourists are generally concerned only with wards within these
districts of Tokyo. It is therefore advisable to note the following
details:
Ikebukuro, Shinjuku, Asakusa, Ginza and Shibuya for night-life
(every sort of entertainment).
Akasaka, near the large hotels, for evenings.
Marunouchi, because that is where many large banks and firms
have their head offices.
Ginza for its shopping street.

Administration

Tokyo is governed by a council with 126 members and a chief
mayor or governor who is elected for four years.

Population and Religion

Population

As early as 1758 Tokyo, then called Edo, became the largest city
in the world with its population of 1·4 million people. But for
centuries Tokyo was in no way a cosmopolitan metropolis,
because Japan was an island kingdom shut off from the rest of
the world. Of the 2·7 million houses in the city of Tokyo more
than a million have less than 270 sq. ft (30 sq. m) floor space
per dwelling. Because people in Tokyo came from different
parts of Japan and from different family backgrounds, there is
less community spirit here than one would find in other towns
and villages in Japan.
The city has attracted people from all parts of Japan. They came
here in the hope of finding, in particular, better employment
prospects. In this great melting pot there are nowadays only a
few genuine Edokkos, people who have been resident in Tokyo
for at least three generations.
There are some 114,000 foreigners resident in Japan. Most of
them, however, are Koreans who were born here but have not
been able to acquire Japanese nationality.
Foreigners (Gaijin) are still few and far between here. Most are
business men or journalists who are just birds of passage.

People in Tokyo

Burakumin

The origin of "Burakumin" is complicated. During the Edo period, when the "Bushi" or top ranking "caste" were becoming poorer and had to borrow money from the "Shonin" or "merchant caste", they created a new even lower "caste" called "Burakumin" – who were mainly criminals. These "outcastes" were allowed to do only menial tasks or jobs that nobody else wanted. Today in the Kanto area (which includes Tokyo) they are scattered and do not live in ghettos as previously. It is said that some of the big Japanese companies keep a register (red book) containing names of "Burakumin", and discrimination has excluded them from professional

11

careers and even excluded them from marrying into the higher (or other) classes. A few years back the Burakumin started to defend themselves against this scornful attitude that society adopted towards them and joined together to demand their rights.

Religion

The two dominant religions are Shintoism, an animistic nature religion, and Buddhism, which has its own particular form in Japan. The two religions do not conflict; the curious result of this is that a survey revealed that 72 million Japanese claim to be Shintoists and 81 million Buddhist, while the total population amounts to over 120 million. Furthermore most weddings are Christian, though most people are buried as Buddhists. Only Japanese nationals can become Shintoists. Christians of various denominations amount to barely 1% of the population.

Buddhist temples are distinguished by swastikas, an ancient symbol, but unlike the "clockwise" swastika of the Nazis, the Japanese swastika, called "manji", is formed anti-clockwise. Shinto shrines can be recognised by the gates ("Torii") made of baulks of timber.

Shintoism

Shintoism is a purely Japanese religion. Until 1945 it was the state religion. It is only practised in this country, and only Japanese can be Shintoists. Until the 6th c. A.D. it was the only religion practised in Japan, and accordingly it did not originally have any particular name. It was only with the introduction of Buddhism that it was called Shintoism, a name derived from the Chinese and meaning roughly "the divine way". Shintoism is an animistic religion, a nature religion whose basis is the belief that nature is peopled by spirits and quasi-divine beings. There are, according to early sources, 800 times 1000 gods or quasi-divine beings.

Among these divinities – it is important not to give the term its western connotations – are mountains (which means that Fuji is a sacred mountain for the Shintoists), and trees, sun and moon, and animals such as snakes, foxes and cranes. These natural forces are "kami" (or higher) beings which are benign and kindly. "Kami" means "Shinto deity", but it also means "a pure mind" for Shintoists. The ancestors become "hotoke" – a kind of living spirit of the dead person(s). There can, however, be "hotoke" of a living person, if really pure, e.g. Mother Theresa of Calcutta would be termed "hotoke" by Japanese. Thus it was that the Yasukuni Shrine in the heart of Tokyo received the souls of all the soldiers who fell in the wars and also those of others who died for the nation (including leaders, doctors and others), not necessarily during a war.

There are different types of religious beliefs within the religion of Shinto, and in one of these the Emperor was until 1945 regarded as the Head of Shinto. He was considered to be the direct successor of the sun goddess Amaterasu-Omikami. For this reason, too, the Shinto clergy were subservient to the throne. The Shinto religion requires, as is in accord with its origins as a nature religion, no fixed faith. It emerged without written rules and regulations, moral precepts or fixed moral code. It is only in the last two centuries that it has gradually developed a general system of ethics.

The most important "kami" are revered in shrines which are generally surrounded by well-tended gardens, themselves another expression of the relationship between this religion

Shinto priest in robes

Buddhist priest

Members of Soka Gakkai

and nature. It is here that the faithful can come and revere his "kami". They may also celebrate their festivals (matsuri); these can either stress the mutual harmony or else help re-create it. Because cleanliness is extremely important for Shintoism – even contact with death is avoided – the faithful pour water over their hands and symbolically purify their mouths before entering the sacred precinct of the shrine.

Even nowadays Shintoism plays a significant role in Japan and the aid of the "kami" is regularly invoked, at seed time and harvest, for instance, when they are honoured throughout Japan in festivities and celebrations.

Buddhism

Buddhism, coming by way of Korea, reached the island kingdom of Japan in A.D. 538. At the time it was violently opposed by the Shinto priests because the Japanese religion which accepted life in all its fullness could not tolerate Buddhism as a "foreign" religion. It was, however, taken up by the upper classes, especially by Prinz Shotoku (574–621), and soon became fashionable at court. Buddhism came to be highly regarded as the expression of a superior, spiritualised culture.

In the course of time Buddhist doctrine took on a Japanese tincture as sects formed, Shintoism interpreted the Buddhist divinities as "kamis" and the Buddha statues as visible links in artistic form between man and "kami". As Shintoism moreover tended to concern itself with this world and Buddhism tends towards the transcendental, Buddhism was eventually accepted as complementary to Shintoism.

As early as the 12th c. the first Japanese form of Buddhism emerged with the development of Amida Buddhism. By the grace of Amida, one of the many incarnations of the Buddha, man could be confident of being born again after death and entering "Jodo" (meaning "enlightenment").

This form of Buddhism met its keenest antagonist in the priest Nitchiren (1222–82), the founder of a sect that took his name. He linked Buddhist doctrine with patriotism, demanded the banning of all other sects and required missionary fervour from his disciples.

A third development of Japanese Buddhism is Zen doctrine. With the rigorous ordering of the practice of meditation and the fundamental disciplines of life in the sect, this was in harmony with the honour code and life style of the Samurai, the Japanese warrior aristocracy. They used the severe meditation exercises as a means to self-discipline, in order to disregard every selfish thought and to learn to cease to fear death, which was the highest stage in self-disregard.

The central point in Zen practice is "zazen" (meditation while sitting). It is reputed to lead to "satori" (enlightenment), a sudden realisation by the faithful of the unity of all being. There is a slight distinction between "satori" and "jodo", both meaning enlightenment. "Satori" is "the reaching of enlightenment", while "jodo" is, in a sense, after "satori", "enlightenment attained".

The disciples have to give their "san-zen" (masters) reports on what they have experienced during meditation. The masters often try to correct (even by means of corporal punishment) the errors their disciples have made. Masters test their disciples' understanding by "koan" (an exchange of question and answer).

These Zen sayings, which have the character of aphorisms, but which incorporate challenging and paradoxical ideas, are intended, in accord with the nature of Zen Buddhism, to be the crystallisation of one basic notion. Some are famous in the West.

A similar poetry is expressed by Zen art and Zen architecture. In painting it is concentration on essentials, with just a few brush strokes, that comes across most clearly. Zen architecture is immediately recognised with its undecorated, simple forms. The tea ceremony, too (see Sights, Tea Ceremony), has its origins in Zen Buddhism.

Soka Gakkai is a sect which was founded in 1930 and restored in 1946. It, too, harks back to the priest Nichiren, and its orientation is strongly nationalistic.

Soka Gakkai is based on the idea posed by Nichiren that religious spirituality and political power must be deeply interpenetrated. Accordingly the sect founded the "Komeito" (the Party for Clean Politics) in 1964. It soon grew to become one of the stronger opposition parties in the two Houses of Parliament, but meantime it severed its links, at least nominally, with the religious movement. It has some 10 million members. They are pledged to unconditional obedience and have to pay large financial contributions. It is virtually impossible to leave, and control is exerted by physical threats by the strictly organised hierarchy of officials.

An estimated 20 million Japanese belong to the Soka Gakkai itself. The sect would like to make its form of Buddhism the state religion and preaches worldwide disarmament and the nationalisation of key industries, all in the pursuit of a new form of Japanese nationalism.

The astonishing popular support of Soka Gakkai is explained primarily by its identification with certain sectors of society. It organises cultural and educational evenings which provide that feeling of togetherness which is so important for the Japanese.

Soka Gakkai

Christianity was brought to Japan in the 16th c., first by the Portuguese and then also by the Dutch. It awakened an echo in the oppressed peasantry who saw much in it that corresponded with their suffering. But as early as 1597 there was persecution of Christians, with over 30,000 losing their lives, some of them after frightful torture. In 1640 Japan was virtually barred to foreigners. It was only in 1873 that exiled Christians were permitted to return and follow their belief freely; in 1889 freedom of religion was promulgated. That is why barely 1% of the population are Christians nowadays. The influence of the Christians on the social and intellectual life of Japan is, however, considerable, not least because of the founding of schools which Christians and non-Christians alike can attend.

Tokyo is the see of a Catholic archbishop.

Christianity

Culture

Tokyo is not just quantitatively the scientific and modern cultural centre of Japan – it is the city which sets the tone for the whole country. Kyoto can be regarded as the real "cultural centre" of Japan.

General

Tokyo is the seat of the Japanese Academy, the Japanese Council for Science and a great number of learned societies. There are more than 200 state, municipal and private universities, polytechnics, colleges and high schools. Among the libraries the National Library is outstanding. The National Theatre is the most important of the theatres, and the National Museum the most famous of the museums. This music-loving city has seven orchestras; the NHK (the Radio Symphony Orchestra) and the Japan Philharmonic Orchestra have the widest international reputations. The support of traditional and modern art is, for the most part, in private hands. Stores, galleries and a number of institutions are particularly concerned with the fine arts.

Tokyo is the place where all the important newspapers are published, and NHK (i.e. Nippon Hoso Kyokai), a public radio station, and most commercial TV companies have their headquarters here.

Universities

If all the state, municipal and private universities and high schools are taken into account the total number amounts to more than 200. Several of them, however, would not be considered to be up to university standard in Europe.

In Japan future career prospects tend to be predetermined by attendance at the "right" university. Selection is on the basis of an examination system which begins at school and which, by European standards, seems to produce an inordinate amount of psychological stress. Students who have passed the examinations in the university of their choice need in addition to pass a "company examination" in order to be considered for a good job.

University of Tokyo

The most respected state university is the Tokyo University, known as "Tokyo Daigaku" and often shortened to "Todai". Many of its alumni go into the civil service. The private universities are extremely expensive. Virtually no students from abroad attend them. Those most worthy of mention here are the Keio and Waseda Universities. Among the private universities is also the United Nations University which was founded in 1972. It is hoped it will one day become a meeting point for international research and teaching. At present the enterprise is not progressing very satisfactorily, because Japanese students prefer the established institutions with whose help they can expect to get on in their careers.

The high schools in Tokyo are well regarded. Among them are the High Schools for the Fine Arts and for Music, the Tokyo University of Arts and the Seiha Ongakuin in Shinjuku.

Tokyo is the educational centre of Japan. So it is naturally here that are found the Japanese Academy, the Japanese Scientific Council and numerous other learned societies which do not, however, open their doors to foreigners. Contacts with other countries are, however, sought and maintained, and there are accordingly a large number of foreign learned societies and institutes in Tokyo.

Learned societies and institutes

Among the Japanese Institutes which have won a world-wide reputation are Tokyo's Nuclear Research Institution and the University of Tokyo's Institution for Aviation and Space Travel.

The Japanese are very conscious of tradition, so it seems obvious to them, in every sphere of activity, whether in sport, dance, music or theatre, that they should practise the forms that have been handed down to them.

Theatres

Accordingly, it is possible to go and see Noh, Bunraku and Kabuki on the Tokyo stage. The performances are virtually always sold out, and the actors are as popular as film stars in the West. At the same time the Japanese are very keen on revues of the Folies-Bergère type. These gorgeously produced shows with their troupes of girls, strip-tease in Western and Japanese style, with sketches and short numbers which are often full of innuendo, always attract large audiences, especially of men.

The Japanese are very fond of such European composers as Beethoven and Mozart. Concert audiences are very well informed and enthusiastic. The inhabitants of Tokyo are, in this, typical of their fellow countrymen.

Concerts

This enthusiasm is reflected in the fact that there are in Tokyo no fewer than six symphony orchestras of international standing – the NHK Symphony Orchestra, the Japan Philharmonic Orchestra, the Tokyo Symphony Orchestra, the Shin Nihon Philharmony Yomiuri Symphony Orchestra, the City Symphony Orchestra and the Tokyo Philharmony.

There are also many choral societies and two opera companies, though they perform only rarely. There is virtually no state support for musical education in Japan. Many performances are simply under the auspices of firms, but these are open to the general public.

Transport

Harbours

Tokyo harbour is part of a port complex extending along Tokyo Bay from Yokohama in the W to Chiba in the E. Freight handled amounts annually to more than 70 million tons, of which about 80% consists of imports. This makes it the seventh most important port in Japan. As for container traffic, Tokyo is at present fifth in the world. The latest available figures were 3853 deep-sea vessels from almost every country in the world, putting in at Tokyo, and 59,729 coastal vessels.

The intensive build up of trade which characterised in particular the period after the Second World War is still continuing unabated. To provide sites for industrial plant which has economic connections with the harbour's trade, the area around the harbour is constantly being increased in size by land reclamation schemes. The disadvantage is the fact that the quality of life is being disturbed by these immense building operations. That is why, as they contemplate expanding the port still further, the municipal authorities are considering plans for "marine parks" which will allow the inhabitants of the city to see the sea once again.

Airports

Tokyo has two major airports. For many years there was only Haneda; nowadays, with the exception of flights by foreign VIPs, it is used only for inland journeys and by flights to and from China.

The international airport is Narita (see Information, Arrival). It lies, however, some 38 miles (60 km) E of the city to which it is linked by bus and rail shuttle services. Although work was completed as early as 1973, it did not come into use until 1978 as the local inhabitants and the environmentalists attempted to prevent its opening by means of demonstrations, often on a gigantic scale, which were sometimes marked with violent conflicts with the police.

The government had dispossessed a number of farmers, some of whom felt they had not been given adequate compensation. The construction of a second runway for arrivals and departures has also been prevented by the opposition of people of the neighbourhood who have received support from all over Japan. As a result Narita Airport is not functioning at full capacity.

Railway

Japan's highly developed railway network is among the most modern in the world.

The broad-gauge Shinkansen line worked by the JNR (Japanese National Railway) links the capital with Kyoto, Osaka, Kobe, Fukuoka, and Sendai. The trains depart every 30 minutes and reach an average speed of 125 mph (200 km/h). The Shinkansen (see A–Z, Shinkansen) is the most important element in Japan's transport system link on the N–S axis. Apart from this railway there is just one road of motorway standard which is generally blocked by traffic jams.

Long distance trains depart from Tokyo Main Station for destinations in SW Japan, from Ueno Station for the N and from Shinjuku for the W.

Underground

The underground, or subway, is the most important form of transport for people within the city of Tokyo (see Information, Public Transport). The network of routes covers over 100 miles (163 km).

Ueno Station concourse

At rush hours (between 7 and 8 a.m. and around 5 p.m.) the trains are desperately overcrowded. Students are employed specially to push and shove the passengers into the coaches so that the doors can be shut. This method, which seems particularly gross and discourteous in a land where people generally like to keep their distance, has its explanation. The vast majority of commuters in Tokyo go from their homes to their place of work by public transport. Some districts of the city are almost completely deserted, which is an indication that the places of work are all concentrated together.

Private railways are another sector of public transport. Their operations are based at Tokyo Main Railway Station and at Shibuya and Shinjuka Stations. The Main Station is, for instance, the terminus of the Yamate Line, a circle line of some 22 miles (34·5 km) which encircles the city centre in two directions and stops at all the major railway stations.

Private railways

Most buses in the city centre are run by the municipality, while those in the outlying districts are under private ownership.
The bus network is very well developed. But using it is so complicated that even locals have problems in coping with it and visitors are best advised to seek other means of transport.

Buses

From Tokyo motorways lead off across the island in all important directions. These motorways are, however, not easy to find, the tolls are high, and at weekends they are so crowded with traffic that generally average speeds are no more than 25 mph (40 km), especially as there are so many goods vehicles.

Motor traffic

Transport

Railway between skyscrapers

Expressway from above

Expressway on concrete piers

In Tokyo itself the traffic is chaotic. In order to by-pass the points where traffic jams regularly built-up on account of the antiquated pattern of streets in the city, so-called expressways on piers have been constructed since 1964. Users are charged a toll, and traffic jams often block them completely.

Commerce and Industry

Tokyo is Japan's major consumer market, partly because of the size of its population and partly because of the wages and salaries which are well above the national average. Tokyo is also the most important commercial city in Japan with the head offices of all the Japanese clearing banks and branches of American and European banks. 66% of all Japanese firms have their headquarters in Tokyo. The Stock Exchange makes the city the absolute financial centre of the country.

Commerce

Tokyo forms part of Keihin, the most important industrial region of Japan; other centres are Kawasaki and Yokohama. The industrial region stretches from Sagami Bay in the S to Maebashi in the N. It is here that the most important Japanese steel plants have been set up, and it is here, too, that shipbuilding and the petrochemical industry have developed, the latter in some cases on specially reclaimed off-shore islands. 32% of Japan's total industrial output is produced in this region. The manufacturing industries are represented by aircraft and automobile construction, machine building and shipbuilding, and electronic, mechanical, pharmaceutical and cosmetic firms. Textiles, leather, paper, food and confectionery are other important industries here. Among the most important business organisations in Tokyo are:
Keidanren, with 750 firms, for the development of all organisations within the economy; it corresponds approximately to the C.B.I.
Nikkeiren, with 500 firms, for the development of employers' organisations.
Nissho, combining 445 chambers of trade and commerce.
There are a large number of private economic enterprises in Tokyo.

Industry

With Japan becoming more and more a country where visitors come from abroad for tourism and for congresses – and in this development Tokyo is in the forefront – the service industries are taking on an ever greater importance. In 1979 alone 16,136 participants came from abroad to take part in congresses in Japan, and that year tourism increased by 7·1%. The hotel and catering trade profited particularly from this upturn as did those industries whose wares are sold as souvenirs and especially those whose products, such as cameras, are famous all the world over.

Service industries

The Government of Japan

Japanese democracy is, as Mr Nakasone, now the Prime Minister, once cried out in parliament, an artificial flower, a cut blossom. By which he implied that it was something that had

The Government of Japan

been forced on Japan by the American Army of Occupation. Political parties came into existence in the course of the present century as a result of an Imperial edict. As for trade unions, they are astonishingly firm in their support of the State and of businesses. This may, in fact, go some way to explaining the success of modern Japan in industry and commerce.

The Constitution was promulgated on 3 November 1946 and came into force on 3 May 1947. Under its provisions the Emperor is Head of State. The legislature is divided into an Upper House (Senate) and a Lower House (House of Representatives). There is universal suffrage for men and women; they all have the right to vote once they are 21 years old.

Head of State

Japan is a parliamentary monarchy. The throne is inherited by the eldest son, according to the principles of primogeniture. The title "Tenno" is an allusion to the Emperor's divine descent. Nowadays, however, the Emperor, who in former times was revered by some people as divine, is simply a symbol of the state and of its people's unity. Under pressure from the Americans, he was persuaded to renounce his personal divinity when he made his New Year Message in 1946. Since then he has ceased to have any political role in the state apart from ceremonial occasions such as the opening of Parliament. Hirohito has been Japan's "Tenno" since 1926.

Since the end of the 1970s there have been numerous attempts to restore the Emperor's "rights". For instance, the Imperial calendar computations were reintroduced, as was the singing of the Imperial hymn each morning in the schools. But basically most Japanese have come to terms with democracy – they appreciate the complete freedom of speech, of the press, etc. – and the parties to the left of the political spectrum in particular – the Socialists and Communists – defend the democratic principle and the Constitution whenever opportunity offers.

Senate (Sangi-in)

The Senate has 252 members (1981). They are elected for a six-year term, half of them coming up for re-election every three years. 100 of the Senators are elected on nation-wide lists, while the remaining 152 Senators are elected on lists prefecture by prefecture.

The last elections took place on 22 June 1980. Since then the distribution of Senate seats has been as follows: 136 Liberal Democrats, 47 Socialists, 27 Komei-to, 12 Communists, 12 Social Democrats, 25 other groups and Independents.

Lower House (Shugi-in)

The Lower House (or House of Representatives) has 511 members. They are elected for a term of 4 years by 123 constituencies and by the island of Okinawa. Between 2 and 5 members are returned by each constituency, depending on its size and population.

Since the election of 22 June 1980 the distribution of seats has been as follows: 286 Liberal Democrats, 106 Socialists, 33 Social Democrats, 34 Komei-to, 29 Communists, 11 Independents and others, and 12 New Liberal Club.

Cabinet

Executive power resides in the Cabinet. It comprises the Prime Minister and the other ministers, who must themselves be Japanese citizens entitled to vote. The Cabinet is answerable to Parliament. The present Prime Minister is Mr Nakasone who replaced Mr Zenko Suzuki after the latter's resignation.

The Prime Minister and half the members of his Cabinet must

be members of parliament. He has the right to form his Cabinet as he considers best. But after a vote of no confidence in Parliament the Cabinet must resign or else the House of Representatives must be dissolved within ten days.

In 1945 the Americans set in train a liberalisation of Japanese political life, reforms ranging from the founding of trade unions to the granting of equal rights to the sexes. Progress has, however, been only hesitant in these spheres. Naturally the changes could not occur overnight when there was no corresponding historical evolution in the same direction. There is a deep-seated and, it might be said, an undemocratic dread of changes in government. The Liberal Democratic Party which has been in power for three decades has profited from this. Besides, what exactly is meant by a "political party" in Japan? During the feudal period the distribution of power in the state was clearly laid down; it was clear who was on top, who at the bottom, and everybody knew his exact place on the ladder.

Democracy has produced a sense of equality with which the Japanese politicians scarcely know how to cope. There is no party in Japan which allows its policies to be determined by a process of consultation between top and bottom and thus become independent of the opinion of individual members of parliament. When it is politically expedient, the number of members of the ruling LDP may well go up from one million to three, but the total falls away again just as rapidly. The LDP, like the other parties, is more or less a coalition of various interest groups which comes together, to the disgust of many voters, and forms a block, forgetting the mandate given by the electorate. Because no device is neglected in this never-ending power-struggle, corruption sometimes rears its ugly head, but it is not overt or rife as in many Asiatic countries. In 1973 Prime Minister Tanaka had to resign after the discovery of his involvement in a gigantic scandal with Lockheed. His successors, too, have, if in rather different fashions, come under suspicion of bribery.

Japanese Parliamentary life does not have the same appearance as that found in the Western democracies. There are no great debates here, no decisive votes. Because each party is first obliged to go through the long and wearisome process of reconciling all its own various interest groups, most political differences are in fact settled in secret. The sole exception are the Communists. As early as 1965 they followed the pattern of the Euro-Communists and are prepared to raise radical issues in Parliament. That is, however, widely regarded as gross and un-Japanese, and the media generally condemn this "extravagant" behaviour.

A politican who goes to extremes or even commits serious blunders need not be afraid of losing his position on that account. The principles of loyalty and faithfulness which have been inherited from the Samurai outlook will work positively to his advantage. For instance, Matsuno, the Minister of Defence, was obliged to confess to having pocketed 500 million Yen in an armaments scandal. All the same he was re-elected, because the voters simply would not abandon a man to whom they had pledged their loyalty. A consequence is that in the Japanese Parliament the proportion of elderly members is far above the average. Not to re-elect them would amount to the disgraceful crime of disloyalty.

Parties

Parliamentary life

The interplay of political and
social forces

As this account reveals, the system of government is strongly marked by its formality. The Cabinet headed by the Prime Minister and with some twenty other members is responsible to Parliament. But open debate before the public eye remains something very rare. Gradually, however, and equally unnoticed, a compromise is also reached between the claims of various social groups. Japan is famous for the way opposing forces within a firm or authority only come to a decision after long debate. That reflects, however, not only a taste for the democratic process but also because each person, who after consideration of the matter is not entirely convinced, is looked on as a potential source of disharmony who is best conciliated in advance. This is also the way the government treats industry, banks and business: they all get a hearing at the Cabinet, and equally representatives of government attend meetings of the business organisations. In the final analysis all important decisions are reached collectively, and that no doubt is Japan's source of strength in the world's markets. In Japan meanwhile fringe groups are generally kept in their place.

Famous People

Matsuo Basho
(1644–94)

The Japanese poet Matsuo Basho was the master of the typical Japanese art of the "Haiku", a verse form which consists of a single stanza of three lines and just seventeen syllables altogether (see Quotations). The full meaning of lyrics in this form is revealed only when it is appreciated how much is just implied.

Suzuki-Harunobu
(1725?–29 June 1770)

The master Harunobu was born in Tokyo. He is considered the first classical master of the coloured woodcut, making a significant contribution to the development of polychromatic printing. In his coloured woodcuts the elegant female figures with their graceful limbs, such as his "Beauties of Yoshiwara", are especially impressive. His pictures of children and intimate erotic prints are fascinating with their discreet charm.

Ando Hiroshige
(1797–12 Oct. 1858)

The painter Hiroshige was born and died in Tokyo, then called Edo. He is particularly revered as a master of the coloured woodcut.

Hiroshige became very well acquainted with the Japanese landscape as a result of his extensive travels through the country. He portrayed Japan as he saw it in every mood at every hour of the day and every season of the year. His knowledge of European painting is reflected in his artistic and, to some degree, starkly asymmetrical coloured woodcuts.

Hiroshige's most famous series of woodcuts are: "Views of the Capital of the East" (1830); "Famous Sites in Kyoto" (1834); "Eight Views of Lake Biwa" (1834–5); and most important of all, "53 Views of Tokkaido Route".

Kondo Isami
(1834–69)

Kondo Isami was an unscrupulous mercenary, who raised a private army against the Emperor. He was defeated in a decisive battle in what is now the Ueno district of the city. When he was captured, his throat was cut.

Oishi Yoshio Kuranosuke avenged the death of his lord, Asano Takuminokami, whom a villain had denounced. For years he pretended to be indifferent and kept his peace; finally, together with 46 other Samurai he took his revenge. These 47 Samurai have become paragons of absolute loyalty in Japan. Their graves (see A–Z, Sengakuji Temple) are still visited nowadays and joss-sticks are burned in their honour.

Oishi Yoshio Kuranosuke (1659–1704)

Yukio Mishima is one of the few Japanese authors to have achieved world-wide fame. He modernised the classical Noh plays, which aroused considerable controversy. Mishima could not endure it when his country adopted democratic forms of government after the Second World War, and he bitterly regretted the collapse of tradition. By that he meant above all the Samurai spirit and their unconditional loyalty to their lord, which in this case meant the Imperial dynasty. With the help of a private army of fanatics he tried to organise resistance to developments which he felt were un-Japanese and decadent. His actions did not win him many friends, and so he committed Harakiri, the classical Japanese form of suicide.

Yukio Mishima (1925–70)

Moronobu, a painter and master of the woodcut, devoted his energies primarily to the portrayal of social life, with genre pictures and studies of modern beauties. He illustrated many books in black and white and, by producing the first single-sheet prints, he established the woodcut as an independent art form. Moronobu taught in Edo where he also died.

Hishikawa Moronobu (1618?–94)

Raiden was a Sumo wrestler who weighed 370 lb. He threw virtually all his wrestling opponents and lost only 10 of his 264 bouts. The world of Sumo wrestling has never known anything else like this record. Visitors who see with what enthusiasm the Japanese follow the fortnight-long Sumo tournament (see A–Z, Sumo) will appreciate that Raiden is still not forgotten.

Raiden (1767–1825)

Kenzo Tange is perhaps Japan's most important architect. He designed several government buildings and museums. He is responsible for St Mary's Catholic Cathedral and the daring design of the swimming pool put up for the 1964 Olympics. In his architecture he combines traditional building techniques, such as were used for the temples, with modern materials.

Kenzo Tange (b. 1913)

History of Tokyo

There was a marshy, wooded area where present-day Tokyo now stands. It was occupied by a warrior family which was presumably called Edo. This name was later given to the city before it became Tokyo.

12th c.

Construction of the first stone fortress when General Ota builds Edo Castle.

1457

The Feudal Lord Tokugawa makes the insignificant fishing village the provincial capital.

1590

The Emperor makes Ieyasu Shogun (or Field Marshal) with the duty of stopping foreign barbarians invading the country. As

1603

Shogun he seizes political authority, reducing the Emperor who resides in Kyoto to a mere semi-religious symbolic figure. Under the Shogunate of the Tokugawa dynasty Edo grows and becomes a large city. Craftsmen, traders, officials, artists and warriors are attracted to the Shogun's court. For the next 264 years of the Tokugawa period power lies with the aristocracy. Japan shuts itself off from the outside world.

1634	The Shogun commands all Daimyos (feudal magnates) to reside with their families in Edo. The object is to ensure the loyalty of the magnates to the Tokugawa dynasty.
1635	From this year on all the Daimyos have to undertake a period of attendance at court in Edo.
1657	Almost half the city is laid waste by a catastrophic fire. Reconstruction begins immediately.
1705	With its 1·1 million inhabitants Edo is larger than London.
1707	Fuji erupts. It rains down ash, even on the streets of Edo.
1853	A U.S. naval squadron under Matthew Perry puts in at Shimoda. In the name of the American President Fillmore he demands the opening of Japan to foreign trade. At first, by the Kanagawa Treaty, the ports of Shimoda and Hakodate are opened for trade with foreigners; then other ports are declared open. Japan decides to modernise, to catch up with the West.
1868	The Imperial dynasty wins back its authority. The last Shogun of the Tokugawa dynasty is forced to abdicate. The Emperor with his family and court moves to Edo. The city is proclaimed the capital of Japan, and its name is changed to Tokyo. The Meiji Period begins with the Emperor Matsuhito.
1869	The first telegraph link between Tokyo and Yokohama is inaugurated.
1871	The postal system is introduced.
1872	The first rail link between Tokyo and Yokohama is inaugurated. The European calendar is introduced.
1912	Emperor Matsuhito dies. The Meiji Shrine is built in his honour. With its extensive grounds it becomes one of the symbols of Tokyo.
1914–18	Japan fights alongside the Allies in the First World War. It captures the German garrison in Tsingtau (China).
1923	More than 140,000 in Tokyo lose their lives as a result of the great earthquake in the Kanto region. Nearly all the major buildings are destroyed, as well as up to 700,000 dwellings, mainly by the fires that raged after the earthquake. The city is rebuilt in the record period of $7\frac{1}{2}$ years.
1926	Hirohito becomes Emperor.
1930	Tokyo's population has grown to 2,070,913.

After boundary changes Tokyo's population reaches the new record of 6,369,919.	1941
The "Prefecture" of Toyko is proclaimed "Tokyo Metropolitan Area".	1943
Tokyo becomes an inferno. On 9 March the Americans launch an air attack on Tokyo with 300 Flying Fortresses, each with a load of 7–8 tons of bombs. 700,000 bombs lay waste the city which, as the wind whips up the fires, becomes a sea of flames. 197,000 people are killed or reported missing.	1945
Tokyo is rebuilt on its former lines since a commission of experts comes to the conclusion that the population will in no circumstances exceed 3·5 million.	1946
Tokyo Tower is built; at the time it is the tallest free-standing tower in the world.	1958
Tokyo hosts the XVIIIth Summer Olympics.	1964
The population of Tokyo exceeds 10 million.	1965
Sunshine City, with 60 storeys and 792 ft (240 m) high, is built in Ikebukuro. It is the highest building not only in Japan but in all Asia.	1978
Pope John Paul II stops in Tokyo during his visit to Japan.	1981

Quotations

"The Japanese appear to be content and a very happy race, apart from one thing – every one of a certain rank carries two terrifying swords in his belt. One of these two swords is a heavy, two-handed weapon, sharply pointed and with an edge as keen as a razor; the other is somewhat shorter . . . The climate is magnificent. The capital city itself is some twenty miles across, and its population is probably several million. Tokyo can moreover boast of something which no European city possesses – delightful roads that fan out in every direction from the city centre and pass over wooded slopes, smiling valleys and shady avenues . . . It would be virtually impossible to besiege the city except with an army the size of the one Xerxes commanded."

Rutherford A. Alcock
First British Consul General
in Japan

With each puff of wind
The butterfly is alighting
Differently there

Matsuo Basho
(1644–94)
Haiku poet

The mountain village
Is cheered at the daytime's close
As plum trees blossom

By light of new moon
The land is inundated
With buckwheat blossom

Quotations

François Caron,
French traveller

(In the 17th c. François Caron made some remarkable observations on the way Japanese builders in Edo, i.e. Tokyo, were prepared to sacrifice themselves for the good of the whole enterprise.)

"If a lord orders the building of a wall, either for the king or for himself, then his servants often beg the privilege of being allowed to be buried beneath it. For their opinion is that no misfortune can befall anything which is built over human flesh. If they are granted the boon they seek, they go happily to the appointed spot and lie down there, allow the foundation stones to be placed upon their bodies and are immediately crushed to death by the weight."

James Clavell
Shogun
(from a novel)

"Mura had not only learnt the arts of Judo and Karate years before but he had also become used to handling a sword and a spear. That was at the time when he had fought for Nakamura, the peasant general, the Taiko, when peasants still might have been Samurais, and Samurais peasants or craftsmen, or even lowly shopkeepers, or else even Samurais once again. It was odd, reflected Mura absentmindedly, that almost the very first thing the Taiko did on coming to power was to give the order that all peasants should cease forthwith to be warriors and should hand in their weapons. The Taiko had forbidden them ever to carry weapons and had set up an inviolable caste system which now regulated strictly every aspect of the Empire's life. The Samurais were paramount, beneath them came the peasant, then the craftsmen; still lower were the shopkeepers and beneath even them the actors, outlaws and bandits; right at the bottom were the Eta, who were not really regarded as human at all because they had to do with corpses, were tanners and fellmongers, and also had to serve as executioners, branders and mutilators. It was, of course, obvious that barbarians were not considered to fit anywhere into this pyramid."

Kaibara Ekiken
Japanese poet

"Heaven and earth know the rest and the turmoil of the tempest and the thunder, and yet nature knows about harmony and quiet."

"If misfortune and illness are rife among men, they too are subject to change and give way finally to happiness and contentment."

The author Hans Kirchmann
on Tokyo

"Tokyo is a moloch, a monster, a nightmare in the guise of a city and a disappointment, in the opinion of many who turn their backs on the city after a short unsatisfactory visit. But Tokyo has to be discovered, and unless you know the language of Japan that is by no means easy. Not only do foreigners easily get lost in the maze of little streets, none of which have names, but they are also soon confused by all Japan's different customs and odd ways.

Certainly Tokyo is not a beautiful city. It is flat, monotonous, crowded, noisy, lacking in outstanding architecture of the sort commonly found in major European cities. But Tokyo is also a friendly city where everybody smiles and likes to be helpful when he meets some Gaijin (or foreigner) who is all at sea. It is possible to stroll around late at night with a briefcase without fear of attack, for crime is rare here. It is only here that the story could be told of the traveller who simply could not manage to get rid of a broken umbrella: he left it in one place, laid it down in another, finally shoved it into a litter bin; but the umbrella followed him all round Japan, sent on after him by friendly souls who simply could not conceive that he was simply no longer interested in having his umbrella.

Visitors coming to Japan who are content just to see the sights that are listed here will not discover the real Tokyo. To do that, you have to get lost deliberately, wander up and down the little streets, seeing how even in front of the smallest houses, which an EEC document scornfully describes as 'rabbit hutches', flowers and shrubs are carefully tended in pots. Visitors must see for themselves how the shopkeepers open their shops in the morning and first stand there in the doorway chatting with their neighbours. They must hear how, amidst the roar of the traffic, old men play on bamboo pipes and see how children try to capture moths and butterflies in nets. Tokyo has lots of delightful nooks and crannies, and there is no way of getting to know these if you insist on going everywhere by taxi.

Tokyo is a new city, yet perhaps not a modern one. At all events, it is a place where old Japan always lies just around the corner. It is hard to love Tokyo as you might love Rome or Paris. That would need too much trouble and money, and there remains too much that is incomprehensible. But visitors will find here pictures and little scenes of daily life which are delightful and quite unique."

"What you need in Japan is patience, whether for the everlasting stopping and starting in the Tokyo traffic jams or for work with and among the Japanese generally.

If the Japanese were not so patient, so unaggressive, so deferential in their dealings with one another, Tokyo, a city with 12 million inhabitants, would have burst apart long ago.

Here where there are 22,500 people to the square mile (15,000 to the sq. km) and each individual has not even so much as one square yard (1 sq. m) each, the 'nastiest city in the world' has a remarkable amount of ambiance.

Good heavens, what dreadful things are written about Tokyo – 'monster' is one of the kindest names it is called, and some see it as a great city whose collapse is just a question of time. But, my dear fellow, we two shan't live to see it.

Unless, that is, you are thinking of the massive earthquake which is foretold with such splendid regularity. According to the figures, there are 500 earthquakes every year in Japan, but only 50 of them are significant to human beings. Even in Tokyo the ground usually trembles about once a month. And the Japanese, being pragmatic, have calculated that an earthquake as strong as that of 1923 would devastate half the city and cause several million deaths."

Peter Krebs
ARD reporter in Tokyo

In spite of everything that comes in the way of a stream in spate, all the waters which part to go round banks and snags finally join together once again and rejoice.

Manyoshu
Japanese poet

On red carnations
The whiteness of butterflies –
Who gave them their souls?

Shiki
Japanese poet

Right in the middle
Mount Fuji reaches the skies:
Japan's spring has come.

Sho-u
Japanese poet

Quotations

Lorenz Stucki
(1925–81)
Japan's hearts beat to
another rhythm

"As far as I am concerned, Tokyo is the most human great city that I know . . . The village lives on behind and next to the office block. The little fish shop, the little greengrocer's, the little butcher's shop, the pharmacy and the little snack bar where you can eat 'Yakitori' (little roasted portions of chicken) or the mini-fish restaurant which can only take seven diners – these all help replace the impersonality of a great city with intimacy. There are few customers and scarcely any shop assistants who, despite their shy reserve, do not pause for a moment's chat. Even when communication is no more than a few words and a shy smile the other person is never just a statistic, but rather a fellow human being, and that is shown again and again in little things. For instance, my broken camera strap is sewn up for me in a photographic shop, and all payment is refused. Or on another occasion, when I buy a bottle of whisky I am given a glass, and in a restaurant I am presented with a saki beaker. People even round down the official price of your purchases, just because they feel like it.

Apart from a few districts entirely built up with shops and banks, even in overcrowded Tokyo, in the lanes behind the high-street façades, people always have a little piece of nature close to them. The front garden may be only a couple of square yards, but in it you can see one or a number of dwarf fir trees, bamboos or an azalea growing amidst a few natural stones. From a bamboo pipe a foot long water splashes into a basin no bigger than a wash bowl set in the grass amidst toy rocks. An alleyway between two wooden houses and scarcely wide enough for a man to pass leads into a secluded courtyard with a cherry tree where a sign hanging from a lamp standard shows the way to a café. Likewise, just a couple of minutes away from the Underground Station in the main shopping street with its four and six lanes of traffic, you come upon a little Shinto shrine or Buddhist temple in a tiny park.

Even in districts such as Marunouchi or Yurakucho, from whose cement, concrete and plate-glass landscape every trace of Japanese feeling seems to have been eliminated, visitors will be amazed if only they pause to look behind the scenes. In the cellar, perhaps, or even in the second or third basement there will be four, five and even more doll's house restaurants, generally fitted out in wood, bamboo, bark and paper, all different in character and in their gastronomic specialities, and catering discreetly for their regular patrons . . .

There is a weekly bulletin, 'Tour Companion', published specially for tourists and available free of charge in all the hotels frequented by foreigners. Each week there is the same little article on Tokyo; it begins with the words 'Toyko is a monster, but it is a safe place to be.'

Tokyo surely must be the only place in the world where you can go for a walk at night in the lanes and alleys with a lot of money on you without having any cause for anxiety. Likewise you have nothing to fear in a crowded store."

Zen poetry

"What is the lotus flower before it is visible on the water?"
"A lotus flower."

"And what is it when it is visible on the water?"
"A lotus flower."

30

Tokyo from A to Z

Akasaka Palace

D4/5

The Akasaka Palace which stretches as far as the Outer Garden of the Meiji Shrine (see entry) was built in 1909 for the Crown Prince. Since 1974 it has been used for the accommodation of State guests.
It was modelled on London's Buckingham Palace, but parts of it are reminiscent of Versailles.

Underground Station
Yotsuya (Chuo Line)

*Akihabara (City District)

F3

This is Tokyo's Electronic City. In the little lanes here there are vast numbers of shops selling recorders, radios, microphones and television sets. There are large stores, too, many with one storey specifically catering for the needs of customers from abroad, but most appliances can be used only in Japan, because the power supply here is 100 volts AC. As the sales staff here includes enough people who can at least explain technicalities in English it is not difficult to discover what can be exported into which country.
Akihabara is in any case well worth a visit because it reveals how keenly the Japanese "play" with all sorts of electronic products.

District
Chiyoda-ku

Railway Station
Akihabara (Keihin–Tohoku Line; Yamanote Line; Chuo Line)

Akasaka Palace

Asakusa Kannon Temple

Pleasure-seekers in front of the Asakusa Kannon Temple

Asakusa Kannon Temple   G2

Location
Asakusa

Railway Stations
Asakusa (Ginza Line), Ueno

Asakusa was once a marshy district and therefore the part of the city where the poor people lived. Even today it is still the place where the old traditional life style is maintained. At the end of a long street of shops where masks, carvings, combs made of ebony and wood, toys, kimonos, fabrics and precious paper goods are on sale, stands the Kannon Temple. It is the centre of Asakusa. Around it, everywhere within the 50 acre (20 ha) temple precinct, there is a warren of lanes with little temples, booths and also places where the Japanese can indulge their passion for betting, especially on horse races. All the streets here are without names.

Kannon Temple

The Temple is dedicated to Kannon, the Buddhist goddess of compassion. It has been here since the foundation of the city. Although the buildings have been destroyed several times, they still retain their original appearance because they have been restored authentically after each catastrophe. Examples of this are the main hall and the scarlet pagoda.

According to legend the Temple was founded in 628 (or more likely in 645) by three fishermen who had found a statuette of the goddess in their nets when they hauled them. In its honour they founded the Temple.

The main entrance is the Kaminari-mon Gate, with a 10 ft (3·3 m) high red paper lantern, weighing 220 lb (100 kg), with an inscription on it meaning "Thunder Gate".

Shrine in the Asakusa Kannon Temple

Incense vat in the Asakusa Kannon Temple

Bunraku

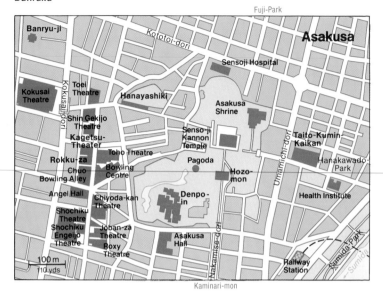

The Asakusa Shrine, known as Sanja-sa-me, was founded by Tokugawa Iemitsu (1604–51) in memory of the three fishermen. In the courtyard in front of the main temple stands the famous and much-loved Incense Vat which is reputed to drive away ailments. Sick people need only to cup their hands around the smoke and apply it to the part of their body which is unwell.

The temple doves are considered to be Kannon's sacred messengers. Nowadays they also tell fortunes if that is what the visitor desires. With its beak a dove pulls out from a heap of cards the one which foretells the enquirer's future.

Asakusa Kannon Temple is one of the most popular in Tokyo. Accordingly the annual festival of Sanja Matsuri (19 and 20 May) is the largest in the city, others being the Sanno Matsuri at the Hie Shrine (see entry) and the Kanda Matsuri at the Kanda Myojin Shrine (see entry).

---

*Bunraku (Puppet Theatre)

Performances
National Theatre 13,
Hayabusacho, Chiyoda-ku.
Tel. 265–7411

Japanese Puppet Theatre – Bunraku – reached its apogee in the 18th c. Like Kabuki theatre (see entry), its roots are Chinese, but in Japan it became a popular form of theatre. In Bunraku either marionnettes worked by strings are used or else very large 4 ft (120 cm) puppets which are carried about and moved by actors. The latter are generally dressed in black, because the public is supposed not to see them. The plays are usually based on ballads. Critics see the highest achievement of Japanese theatre in Bunraku.

Bunraku performances are given only in the National Theatre, and then only for four fortnight seasons each year. Each day there are two performances. For the dates, consult the Tourist Information Centre (see Practical Information, Tourist Information). Tickets can be obtained through hotels or from booking offices (see Practical Information, Box Offices). A suggestion – it is best to get a seat as far forward as possible so that you can really get a good view of the wonderfully crafted puppets.

City Hall   F5

Tokyo's City Hall stands just a few minutes' walk away from the Main Railway Station. Built by the Japanese architect Kenzo Tange, it is the seat of Tokyo's municipal government.
In front of the building there stands a bronze statue of the Feudal Lord Dokan Ota (1432–86) who built Chiyoda (Edo) Castle, now the Imperial Palace (see entry), and who is considered the founder of Tokyo.

Location
Marunouchi

Railway Station
Main Railway Station

Fortune Tellers

The fortune tellers are one of the real sights of Tokyo. It is above all in the evenings that you become aware of them as they set up their booths in the shopping centres. Palmistry and the casting of horoscopes are especially popular.
The fortune tellers play a dominant role in Japanese everyday life. They are consulted on all matters concerning family life and business affairs. In particularly difficult cases they will even visit homes and hang up magical formulae, in order to get a refractory daughter back on the right path for instance.
Astrology and fortune telling are officially recognised in Japan. For the 1980 parliamentary elections the government paid a large sum to have the right day – a lucky day – predicted. In fact on the day it had the good fortune of an overwhelming victory at the polls.

Fuji-san (Fujiyama)

Fuji-san is Japan's sacred mountain and is revered as a goddess. The Army pays no heed to this, however, and firing exercises are regularly carried out here.
Fuji-san is 12,390 ft (3776 m) high and is among the most famous mountains in the world. It is generally shrouded in clouds, and it is only rarely that it is glimpsed in its dazzling whiteness. Those visitors who see this are indeed lucky and will never forget the sight.
Every year some 100,000 Japanese climb up to the volcano which last rained down ash over Tokyo in December 1707. Visitors who wish to climb Fuji-san during their stay in Tokyo must allow for a two-day excursion, and it is only possible to do this during the period between the end of June and the beginning of September.
Sunrise on the summit of Fuji-san is reputed to be among the most impressive of all natural experiences. It is also said that anyone who has had this experience acquires a deeper

Railway
from Shinjuku (JNR Express Train) to Fujiyoshida

Bus Routes
Hammatsucho Bus Terminus; Shinjuki Bus Terminal (up to 5th Mountain Station)

Location
44 miles (70 km) S (Tomei Express Way; Route 138)

Fuji-san

Fuji-san – Japan's sacred mountain

understanding and stronger sensibility of the expressive qualities of Japanese landscape painting.

Six mountain paths, each with ten stopping places, lead up Fuji-san. All these paths are well worn and disfigured with litter, though more and more heed is being paid to the need to keep the landscape clean and tidy. The steady stream of people making their way up the mountain shows the way clearly. Generally pedestrians start from the fifth stopping place. It is also possible to go up as far as the seventh stopping place on horse-back. But the path is steep!

An alternative, which is recommended, is to go on up from the fifth stopping place in the evening and to walk on through the night. A third variant is to climb up by day and spend the night in one of the primitive cabins in the vicinity of the summit, and then visitors can simply wait for the first rays of sunlight in the morning.

Visitors are also recommended to combine routes, climbing up from Fuji-Yoshida, or alternatively starting from Gotemba, and taking the E route for the journey down.

This way leads down into a lava field – beware of falling scree and stones. From the third stopping point there is a bus connection with Route 138 where it is possible to take the service bus to Fuji-Yoshida.

Visitors wishing to climb Fuji-san should see they are suitably dressed before setting out. Because of the ash stout shoes are essential. Warm, wind-proof clothing is an absolute necessity: even in the summer months there can be frost on the summit, and the weather changes very quickly. A sun-hat and a flash-lamp are also required, as is a supply of food (though provisions can be bought in the cabins).

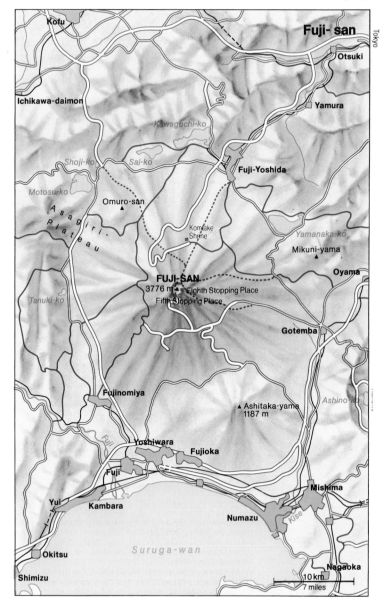

Fuji- san

Tokyo

Kofu

Otsuki

Ichikawa-daimon

Yamura

Kawaguchi-ko

Shoji-ko

Sai-ko

Fuji-Yoshida

Motosu-ko

A s a g i r i - p l a t e a u

Omuro-san ▲

Komitake Shrine

Yamanaka-ko

Mikuni-yama ▲

Oyama

FUJI-SAN
3776 m ▲

Tanuki-ko

Eighth Stopping Place

Fifth Stopping Place

Gotemba

Ashino-ko

Fujinomiya

▲ Ashitaka-yama
1187 m

Fuji

Yoshiwara

Fujioka

Fuji

Mishima

Yui

Kambara

Kise

Numazu

Okitsu

S u r u g a - w a n

Nagaoka

Shimizu

10 km

7 miles

Ashi Lake with Fuji-san

Outward journey

One more word about the outward journey.

The JNR Express train plies between Shinjuku and Fuji-Yoshida. Sometimes passengers have to change trains in Otsuki. From Fuji-Yoshida buses run to the fifth stopping point on the mountain.

It is also possible to travel direct to the fifth stopping point on Fuji-san by bus direct from Tokyo, or more precisely from Hamamatsucho and Shinjuku.

The Hamamatsucho Bus Terminal is housed in the World Trade Centre Building (1st floor), directly opposite the JNR Hamamatsucho Railway Station.

The Shinjuku Bus Terminal is in the Vasuda Seimei 2nd Building (W side), some two minutes' walk from the W exit of the JNR Shinjuku Railway Station. Seat reservations, etc. can be made at the Japan Travel Bureau (see Practical Information, Travel Agents).

Geishas

Agency
Okiya Union
Tel. 583–5459

According to some people the Japanese Geishas are prostitutes of noble birth. Others say they are artistic solo entertainers who play plucked instruments, sing and intersperse their performance with witty conversation. The truth lies somewhere between.

When translated the word "Geisha" means "person of the arts". A Geisha is a woman who has studied for years on end the arts of musical performance, dancing and studied conversation. The most important of the some 60,000 Geishas in Japan are as famous as film stars and earn as much as managing directors. Geishas may be recognised by their external appearance. They dress in expensive kimonos, their hair style is elaborate, their faces are made up white, and they walk with a quite peculiar gait. Their function, in the aloof, man-orientated Japanese society in which women stay at home, is to create a pleasant, relaxed atmosphere on such occasions as social evening meals and so on. The Geishas are trained for their vocation, mainly in Geisha houses. At first they work as "minarai" or "oshaku", that is as maids who serve the wine and food, sing and dance, but are not yet allowed to take part in conversation.

At the end of their training they either work for an agency which finds them engagements, or on their own account. Geisha parties are expensive and exclusive, but they still constitute an important element in the traditional Japanese life style.

Evening sightseeing tours of the city (see Practical Information, Sightseeing) include a visit to a Geisha party.

* *Ginza   F5

Ginza is Tokyo's most famous shopping centre. Lined by exclusive shops and imposing palatial stores which sell literally everything that can be obtained anywhere in the world, in the area there are many tea and coffee shops, cafés, bars and restaurants. At weekends, when everything is open, it is a shopper's paradise because traffic is barred. Gigantic advertising panels on many buildings bathe Ginza in bright light in the evenings. The crowds of moving people carry the visitor along with them, and the din is almost frightening.

Here lie – within the precinct of the shopping street – the Kabuki-za Theatre in which Kabuki performances (see entry) take place, as well as the Shimbashi Embujo Theatre in which the traditional Azuma-odori dances or Bunraku performances (see entry) may be seen. The Ginza district was the commercial centre of the country in the Edo period. It was here that the Chonin, craftsmen and merchants lived. In 1612 Tokugawa Ieyasu had the silver mint (in Japanese "ginza") moved to Edo (present-day Tokyo), and it was sited S of the Kyobashi bridge. At that time Nihombashi was the point where five highways led out into the countryside – the Oshu Road to Sendai, the Nikko Road to Nikko, the Tokaido Road to Kyoto, the Koshu Road to Kofu and the Nakasendao Road to Nagano.

District
Chuo-ku

Railway Station
Yurakucho (Keihin–Tohoku Line; Yamanote Line)

Underground Station
Ginza (Marunouchi Line; Hibiya Line)

*Gokukuji Temple   D2

The Gokukuji Temple is one of the largest temple complexes in Tokyo. It belongs to the Buzan School of the Shingon Sect.

The Temple is dedicated to the goddess Kannon whose statue is reputed to be of Indian origin. Among the treasures of the Temple are a Mandara which is said to date from the Kamakura period (1192–1333). Important personages from recent Japanese history have been laid to rest in the Temple.

Behind the Temple is a knoll which has been the burial place of the Imperial house since 1873. For the Emperor and Empress, however, there are special burial places; these are to be found mainly in Kyoto (see entry) and Nara.

Location
Bunkyo-ku

Underground Station
Gokukuji

Hakone – view of Lake Ashi with Fuji-san beyond

*Hakone

The area of mountains and lakes around the sacred Mount Fuji (see entry) with its volcanic landscape, hot springs and bathing places is a favourite place for the inhabitants of Tokyo on a day out. Particularly at weekends millions pour into this area, and the motorway (Tomei) which leads into it soon becomes one long traffic jam.

The railway goes as far as Yumoto. From here a mountain railway plies to Gora, and then there is a cable car up to Togendai. From near to Togendai it is possible to go by ship from Kojiri along the E bank of Lake Ashi to Motohakone. Thence a bus takes visitors back to Yumoto.

On the Izu peninsula are resorts such as Shimoda and Atami. At weekends they are, however, very crowded.

An alternative round tour: leave Tokyo Main Station by the Shinkansen (see entry) as far as Odawara Railway Station, and go on from there by bus to Motohakone; then continue by bus via Jukkoku-Toge to Atami Railway Station; from there, back to Tokyo by Shinkansen.

From Odawara Railway Station there is the alternative of going by bus as far as Togendai and then, again by bus via the Otome pass, on the Tomei Express Way, back to the Shinkansen Railway Station in Tokyo.

Visitors who prefer not to undertake this excursion on their own on account of possible language problems should go on an organised coach excursion instead (see Practical Information, Travel Agents).

Railway
From Shinjuku (Odakyu Line), from Main Station (Shikansen) to Odawara
Organised circular tours

Location
62 miles (100 km) S

◀ *Ginza – Tokyo's most famous shopping street*

Boat trip on Lake Ashi

An excursion to Hakone is well worthwhile in any case. It should, however, be planned carefully in advance. In particular reservations at hotels should be made before setting out, and it is then possible to arrange to stay overnight in a Ryokan with a thermal spring (see entry).

If the visitor can arrange to undertake this excursion during the week, he will discover a charming facet of Japan and, perhaps, will even have the good fortune to see Fuji revealing its glorious summit, which is usually obscured by mist.

Hamarikyu Park   F6

Railway Station
Shimbashi (Keihin and Yamanote Line)

Opening times
daily 9 a.m.–4.30 p.m.

Hamarikyu Park is ten minutes' walk from Shimbashi Railway Station. Its particular charm is the wonderful view out over the mouth of the Sumida River, the harbour and Tokyo Bay.

The marvellously tended gardens and park with lake and villa ("Garden of the Imperial Hama Villa") were formerly used as the summer residence of the Tokugawa. They are a typical example of the princely gardens of that period, the so-called Daimyo-Teien.

A lagoon spanned by a bridge makes a special impression. After coming into municipal ownership the garden was opened to the public in 1946.

SE of the gardens is the Takeshiba Pier. Steamers for Oshima Island ply from here, and this is the starting point for sightseeing cruises on the Sumida River (see entry).

Happo-En-Park D7

This small, beautifully laid-out park near Meguro Underground
Station has an incredible attraction for wedding couples. When
the lunar calendar shows that the days are favourable there is
a practically endless procession of marriages here. The bride
and groom sit patiently with their families in the hall until their
names are announced over the loudspeakers. The ceremony
itself is short. The preparation and artistic arrangement of the
group photographs takes a good deal longer. Visitors are
welcome to take their own photographs if they wish.

Underground Station
Meguro (Yamanote Line)

Hibiya Park E5

Hibiya Park lies close by the Imperial Hotel, the successor of the
hotel which the famous American architect Frank Lloyd Wright
had built in 1922 and which was pulled down in the 1960s. Its
foundations were placed on rollers, so that it was safe against
earthquake damage. It remains to the present day the premier
Tokyo hotel. (Note: there are toilets in the lower storey of the
present new building.)
Until 1903 Hibiya Park was used for military manoeuvres and
then laid out as a park along European lines. It covers an area
of some 40 acres (16 ha). At midday it is full of people who
come here from the nearby office blocks to eat their lunch in the
open air.
Demonstrations often take place here. Less frequently it is the
site of popular festivals. In November there is a major
chrysanthemum show. Among the buildings in the Park are the
Hibiya-kokaido Concert Hall (see Practical Information,
Music) and the Hibiya Library.

Location
Marunouchi

Underground Station
Hibiya

**Hie Shrine D5

SW of the National Theatre and the Parliament Building (see
entry) and only five minutes' walk from the Akasaka
Underground Station lies the Hie Shrine. (For guests at the
Hilton Hotel it is even easier to reach; it is practically in the hotel
courtyard.)
The shrine, which is also known as the Sanno-sama shrine,
dates from the early Edo period and is dedicated to the divinity
Oyamakui. After being destroyed in the Second World War it
was faithfully restored in 1959.
It is situated on a hill at the foot of which stands a Torii. A zigzag
path leads up to the sanctuary. The divinity Oyamakui used to
be the protector of Kyoto, the former capital. When Ota Dokan
built his palace in Edo (see entry for Imperial Palace) he
nominated Oyamakui as tutelary divinity of his castle. Later
Tokugawa Ieyasu erected this protective shrine in its honour.
Under the Tokugawas the festival of this shrine was among the
most important religious occasions of the capital. Even
nowadays the annual Sanno Matsuri celebrations, between 10
and 16 June, are among the most important in Tokyo. The
culminating point of these is the procession, which takes place
every two years, with the image carried on bearers.

Underground Station
Akasaka (Chiyoda Line)

Hot Springs (Onsen)

There is no form of relaxation on holiday that the Japanese are keener on than bathing in hot springs. They particularly like to do that in the romantic hours of the evening, out in the open air. Japan has many hot springs ("Onsen"), and they are generally skilfully decorated with natural materials, including rocks and ferns.

Either before or after visits to the springs, the bathers consider themselves free to go window shopping or to come to dinner in the lightest attire. The atmosphere is free and easy. There are in fact no hot springs in the metropolis of Tokyo. But they can easily be visited on day excursions, especially in the district of Hakone (see entry).

Ikebana

Where it can be seen
Various Ikebana schools

Ikebana, the Japanese art of flower arrangement, dates back to the 8th c. It developed first at the Imperial Court, where it was practised by ladies but taught by men. Ikebana is governed by fixed aesthetic and philosophical principles which can be distinguished into individual Japanese schools. In the Ikenobo School, which was founded in the 14th c., the prime object is to symbolise in the arranging of flowers the law of Ten-chi-jin, with heaven at the top, earth at the foot, and man in between. In Tokyo there are many Ikebana schools. Visitors are also admitted to their displays (see Practical Information, Cultural Events).

Hot springs

Ikebana: Cherry twigs in the Heika style

Ikebukuro (District)   C1/2

The extension of the Yamanote Line in 1903 did much to further the development of Tokyo's most northerly shopping and pleasure centre. Ikebukuro Railway Station is the centre-point for all transport. Here there is an underground shopping centre (Ikebukuro Shopping Park), the Sunshine City sky-scraper which with its 60 storeys is one of the tallest buildings in Japan. It houses a hotel, an aquarium, a planetarium, etc. Nearby lie an estimated 150 "love hotels", 50 cabarets and theatres and three dozen gaming dens.

Railway Station
Ikebukuro (Yamanote Line)

*Imperial Palace   E4

The chief attraction of the Marunouchi district (see entry) is undoubtedly the Imperial Palace with its parks surrounded by walls and moats (which date from 1613). It is the residence of the Imperial family. The Imperial Palace stands on the site where in 1457 the Feudal Lord Ota Dokan built a first fortress, which served as the focal point from which the city of Tokyo (or Edo, as it then was) gradually spread outwards. After capturing the fortress in 1590, Tokugawa Ieyasu rebuilt it, making it the strongest in the land. Subsequently it was burnt down in a disastrous fire in 1657 and only partially restored. Until 1868 the splendid palace was the residence of the Tokugawa Shoguns. With the restoration of Imperial authority and the transfer of the seat of government from Kyoto to the city which

Location
1–1 Chiyoda
Chiyoda-ku

Railway Station
Main Railway Station

Underground Station
Otemachi

Opening times
Higashi-Gyo Garden:
Tues–Thurs. 9 a.m.–4 p.m.
Palace Garden:
2 Jan., 29 April

had now been renamed Tokyo (i.e. the Eastern Capital), it became the Imperial residence. After destruction in 1873 and again in 1945, the palace has been rebuilt in traditional "flat" style.

The Nijubashi Bridge leads into the interior. Its name, meaning "double bridge", refers to its appearance as reflected in the water. The wall surrounding the palace, which is 7 ft (2 m) thick, is pierced by gates. Of these the S Sakurada-mon was formerly the main Chamberlain's Office, and the Ote-mon, Kirakawa-mon the Kita-Hanebashi-mon are three gates which give access to the East Garden of the Imperial Palace which is open to the public.

Up until the end of the last war it was customary for all passengers on buses passing the palace walls to obey the conductor's order "Kyojo ni!" ("Bow!")

The individual buildings of the Palace are the Main Building (Kyuden), the Residential Building (Fukiage-gosho) and the three Palace Buildings (Kashikodore, Koreiden and Shinden). Within the Palace are to be found a hospital, an air-raid shelter, tennis courts, stables for horses, a cemetery, a paddy field, a kitchen garden, a hen-house and a silk worm farm. Emperor Hirohito also has had a large laboratory installed here for his own research and experiments. The 245 families which make up the Imperial household live in the Palace. Incidentally, Hirohito is pronounced "Hero-heeto" but by the Japanese he is also called tenno heika and the Emperor's name is never used. The Palace is not open to the public; the Palace Gardens are open to the public only on two days in the year, on 2 January and on 29 April (the Emperor's birthday). On these days people flock past in order to catch sight of the Emperor – who lets

The Imperial Palace with its parks – an oasis in a sea of building

Nijubashi – the double bridge in the Imperial Park

himself be seen several times in the course of the day – and to wish him good fortune. On other days permission for a visit must be obtained from the Imperial Chamberlain's Office (Kunaicho). Address: Imperial Household Agency, 1–1 Chiyoda, Chiyoda-ku, Tokyo.

The E Higashi-Gyo-en Garden (or Imperial Palace East Garden) can, however, be visited from Tuesday to Thursday between 9 a.m. and 4 p.m. It has a few old buildings which are worth seeing.

Formerly the Kinomaru Park formed part of the Palace grounds. It is now cut off by the motorway.

In April and October the Togakudo (Music Room) of the Palace is open to the public for the Bunraku and Gagaku performances. To obtain an entry ticket a postcard, with a stamped reply envelope, must be sent to the Imperial Chamberlain's Office (Kunaicho), which is housed in the Sakashita-mon Gate. The exact dates of performances are announced in the newspapers (and information is also available at the Japan Travel Bureau, see Practical Information, Tourist Information).

Japanese Sword Museum   B4

"Kendo-do" (the Way of the Sword) originates, like the tea ceremony, in Zen-Buddhism. Command of this art is supposed to contribute to bodily relaxation and control and to the subduing of the insistent demands of the self.

Sword fighting was originally carried out with genuine swords, though this is no longer the case. With just the most vulnerable

Location
4–25, Yoyogi, Shibuya-ku
Tel. 379–1386

Railway Station
Odakyu Line; Sangubashi

Judo

Opening times
daily (except Mon.)
9 a.m.–4 p.m.

parts of the bodies protected by light armour, the swordsmen attempted to strike one another with two-handed weapons. About 1750 the sword was replaced by less dangerous weapons – bamboo rods, and the "Way of the Sword" replaced "kenjut-su" (or the sword art proper).

Naturally not only does the fighter have to go through a ritual of dedication, but so does his weapon, the sword. The swordsmith was no commonplace blacksmith, but a kind of master of ceremonies. From the very beginning of the art of Japanese sword making – it goes back to the 10th c., the period when the Samurai was beginning to form a distinct caste – the swordsmiths have enjoyed especial respect. The sword with which the Emperor or the Samurai was to win his victories must not be infected by evil spirits. Since the swordsmiths alone knew how to prevent this happening, they had an honoured place in court.

The very act of forging the sword was a rite. The smith avoided all contact with the impurities of the outside world, put on certain special garments for the ceremony of forging the weapon and hung a Shinto rope of straw over the anvil to keep away evil spirits.

Accordingly swords play a large part in Japanese popular mythology. Early sword masters and swordsmiths surpassed even the art of their counterparts in Damascus. It is said that as late as the last century there were cases of Samurai who considered their honour had been infringed and who therefore cut off their opponents' heads or split them open from top to bottom. This story is probably untrue.

The Japanese Sword Museum is a testimony to the reverence with which the sword is regarded. On show are prime exhibits of sword making from both ancient and modern times.

Judo

Training Centre
Kodokan Judo Hall

Underground Station
Korakuen

Opening times
Mon.–Sat. 4–7.30 p.m.

Five million Japanese participate in Judo. It is a combat sport in which the object is to take advantage of your opponent's own strength by being quicker and more adroit. In the course of the last century Japan's police set out to use this art of self-defence as a means of gaining the upper hand over obstinate lawbreakers.

Since then Judo has been practised as a sport all over the world – and is also used by many police forces. The supreme distinction for a Judo fighter is the winning of the Black Belt and with it the highest mastery of Judo.

Judo fans in Tokyo should find their way to the Kudokan Judo Hall where the best Japanese fighters may be seen training on the mats. Practice times are from 4 to 7.30 p.m.

Judo figured for the first time in the Olympic programme when the summer Olympics were hosted in Tokyo in 1964.

**Kabuki

Kabuki is traditional Japanese theatre. It is well worth going to see this medieval, highly skilled and often burlesque theatrical form even if you do not understand one word of what is said. The greatest Kabuki theatre is in Ginza (see entry; for Kabukiza, see Practical Information, Theatres). There performances are given throughout the year.

Kabuki Theatre in the Ginza district

Inside the theatre the scene resembles some enormous family get-together; many of the 2500 spectators bring something to eat, although there are some restaurants around the great auditorium, because the performances last for hours (the shows begin at 11 a.m. and 4.30 p.m.). The spectators stay just as long as they wish – or as long as they can bear to sit – and it is not considered rude to come at any time or to go away when you feel like it.

The word "Kabuki" means roughly "song and dance". In magnificent sets and splendid, valuable costumes the actors perform every sort of emotion with total expression. The stage is often transformed into a cauldron of unbridled passions. After seeing the passers-by on Tokyo's streets who bow so pleasantly and also seem so restrained, visitors can hardly imagine what explosive forces lie hidden beneath the polite masks. The public shares every emotion, weeping, laughing and applauding its heroes thunderously. Shouts of encouragement are for ever ringing out. In times gone by the Kabuki theatre served for the up-and-coming middle classes as a sort of newspaper and gossip-sheet. Scandals and murders were enacted here in epic grandeur. The actors often performed even without a script, with the result that the plot often departed considerably from the reality that had been envisaged. Even nowadays the women's roles are all played by men. Kabuki has nothing in common with the bourgeois culture of European theatre.

In 1645, women were prohibited from performing in the theatres. However, it was reputedly a priestess who made Kabuki popular by her comic improvisation.

**Kamakura

Railway Station
From Tokyo Main Station
(Yokosuka Line) to
Kamakura Station

Location
31 miles (50 km) S

Kamakura lies 31 miles (50 km) S of Tokyo on the Bay of Sagami. It is a favourite seaside resort for the inhabitants of Tokyo and is crowded in July and August. Separated from the hinterland by chains of hills, it has a mild climate and beaches (but the water is not very clean) and offers many opportunities for walks. For tourists it has, however, not much else to offer. In this city, where many artists and writers used to live, there are more than 80 temples and shrines.

Kotokuin Temple

The Great Buddha is especially famous. Cast in 1252 it weighs 100 tons (103 tonnes) and is 40 ft (12·75 m) high, which makes it the second biggest Buddha statue in Japan (the largest being at Nara). In its interior a stairway with thirty steps leads to a window at the back.

The air of calm dignity about this statue is particularly remarkable. The position of the hands symbolises constancy in faith. As early as 1903 Lafcadio Hearn, one of the first foreigners to respect Japanese art, wrote that visitors should on no account miss the opportunity of seeing this Buddha because it gave an impression of the magnificence of Kamakura.

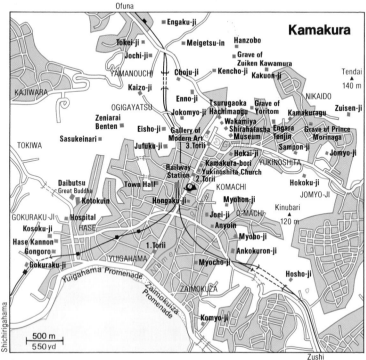

The Great Buddha in Kamakura

Hachimangu Shrine in Kamakura, resting place of the god Ojim

Kamakura

The statue belongs to the Kotokuin Temple which stands in the W part of the city. Formerly it was housed in a hall which was destroyed by a tidal wave in 1495.

Hachimangu Shrine

The Hachimangu Shrine, too, is well worth a visit. This shrine was founded in 1063. In it the legendary Emperor Ojim (3rd c.) is venerated as the god of war (photograph p. 51). The building with its coloured carvings was erected in 1828, while the old Gingko tree with its 23 ft (7 m) circumference in front of the shrine is supposed to be over a thousand years old. On the left of the main hall a collection of portable shrines and weapons is of interest.

Kamakura Matsuri is celebrated here between 9 and 16 April. In the course of this festival there is a display of historical costumes as well as a parade with "Mikoshi" (portable shrines). Furthermore, on the last day a "Yabusame" (or archery contest) is held for riders on galloping horses. Originally it was a competition between courtiers and the Imperial Life Guards. There is another "Yabusame" on 16 September.

Hase Kannon

The Buddhist goddess of compassion is here depicted in a statue over 27 ft (9 m) tall. It is carved from a single camphor trunk.

Zuisenji Temple

Founded in 1327, this temple has a remarkable Zen garden.

In Kita-Kamakura, N of the city, there are four more temples which are worth a visit.

Engakuji Temple

The Engakuji Temple was founded in 1282 by the Regent Tokimune Hojo (1251–84). Delightfully situated in a cedar grove, it is the most ancient Zen establishment in Japan, and it is here that Daisetsu Suzuki, the most famous of the country's Zen teachers, used to live and teach.

The relic hall of the Gautama Buddha, Shariden (built in 1285) and the bronze bell of the temple (cast in 1301) are numbered among Japan's national treasures.

Those interested in participating in meditation exercises in the temple must make arrangements in advance, writing to the following address: Engakuji Temple, Yamanouchi, Kamakura City. Tel. 04 67–22–04 78.

Kenchoji Temple

The Kenchoji Temple was founded in 1253 by the Regent Tokiyori Hojo for Tao Lung – a Chinese monk who is supposed to have brought the four Chinese juniper trees in the courtyard with him. Chinese influence is unmistakable in the architecture (hall, gate).

Ennoji Temple

The statue of a prince of the underworld is the chief attraction in the Ennoji Temple, which was founded in 1250.

Tokeyi Temple

The Tokeyi Temple offered sanctuary to women who had suffered so much in their family or in their relationship with their husband that they fled to the temple. Once they had thrown their sandals over the temple hedge they were considered to have become separated. Accordingly the temple, which was used until 1868 as a nunnery, not inappropriately received the name of "temple of separation".

Engakuji Temple in Kamakura

Kanda   F4

Kanda is famous as Tokyo's bookshop district. There are more than 100 secondhand bookshops in Yasukuni-dori Street, between Surugadai and Kudanshita. That makes Kanda not only Japan's largest bookshop district but one of the largest in the whole world.

Here those who take delight in such things can purchase xylographs (in the Ohya-shobo shop, for instance), buy popular artistic books (in the Sancha-shobo shop, for example), or search for examples of calligraphy (in the Iijima-shoten shop, for example). Works on Japanese and Chinese history can also be discovered (in Isseido's shop and elsewhere).

District
Chiyoda-ku

Underground Station
Jimbocho (Toei–Rokugo Line)

Railway Station
Ochanomizu (Chuo Line)

Opening times
daily except Sun.

Kanda-Myojin Shrine   F3

On a knoll by the River Kanda stands the Shinto Kanda-Myojin Shrine. Its origins are said to date from the 8th c. The present-day, gaily coloured religious building was put up in 1934.

In this shrine Masakado Taira, a knight from the Kanto region, is venerated. In popular belief Taira is the tutelary genius of townsmen.

In front of the gate of the Kanda-Myojin Shrine there is a firm which specialises in Amazake, made from fermented rice, and Koji, a kind of malt.

District
Chiyoda-ku

Railway Station
Ochanomizu (Chuo Line)

The annual Kanda Matsuri festival, celebrated every other year on 14 and 15 March, is, together with the Sanno Matsuri at the Hie Shrine (see entry), among the most important events in the Shinto calendar.

Kimono

Where to purchase
in stores

Modern Japanese women are still keen to wear the Kimono, though it is a garment that is in some respects troublesome. The fair sex attend weddings and other festivals in honour of the family tightly girded and wrapped up in thick layers of clothing. Putting on a Kimono, something which a woman cannot do without help, is an art in itself which has to be learned slowly at special courses. People in Japan like to get married in western hotels, where it is possible to see the garment in all its forms worn, particularly at weekends. Kimonos are, however, expensive, often costing £4000.

Purchasers wishing to acquire at least something resembling this beautiful garment should go to the Kimono department of one of the stores (see Practical Information, Stores) and ask for a Yukata, which can be used back at home as a bathrobe. A pretty Yukata costs between about £25 and £100.

Kodokan Judo Hall

See Judo

Japanese women in traditional Kimonos

Lake in Korakuen Park

*Korakuen Park and Sports Centre   E3

Korakuen Park, one of the most beautiful parks in Tokyo, lies five minutes N of the Railway Station and five minutes S of the Underground Station. It covers an area of 18 acres (7 ha).

Korakuen Park was laid out in 1626 by Tokugawa Yorifusa, ancestor of the Tokugawa branch in Mito. It is the oldest garden in Tokyo. The lake was added later. It was created at the behest of Iemitsu, the third Tokugawa Shogun.

As well as the artistic displays of Japanese and Chinese plants, the little temple on the island in the lake also deserves to be seen. It is dedicated to Benten, the goddess of happiness. the Kantokutei small teahouse has the same name as an old original, larger teahouse destroyed in the 1923 earthquake.

In the E part of the park is the huge Korakuen Games and Sports Centre where there is skating, billiards, table-tennis and swimming, and also the inevitable Pachinko and electronic games.

Foreign films in their original versions are shown in the cheap student cinemas.

District
Bunkyo-ku

Underground Station
Korakuen (Marunouchi Line)

Railway Station
Suidobashi (Chuo Line)

Opening times
daily 9 a.m.–4.30 p.m.

Kuramae Kogugikan

See Sumo.

**Kyoto

Railway
from Main Railway Station
(Shinkansen Line)

Location
365 miles (588 km) SW

The ancient Imperial city of Kyoto is not one of the nearer places for an excursion from Tokyo according to the distance shown on the map. Many attractive spots almost adjoining the capital can only be reached by car, but travelling to them takes a lot of time, especially when the average speed can easily be no more than 15 miles (30 km) an hour. So to recommend a trip to Kyoto is not irrelevant, because you can get there in three hours by the Shinkansen Line (see entry). It is, however, best to plan to spend at least one night there. Visitors can obtain help from the Japan Travel Bureau (see Practical Information, Travel Agents) and from their own hotels concerning organised tours with a fixed itinerary, as well as hotel bookings, etc.

Visitors who cannot speak Japanese will have difficulties in coping with a visit to Kyoto by public transport. It is therefore best to have a list with all the places you wish to visit written out in Japanese in advance and take a taxi. Alternatively visitors can take an organised sightseeing tour. The Tourist Information Centre is on the ground floor of Kyoto Tower, directly opposite the Main Railway Station. An even better idea is to hire a driver and car for the entire day. The price charged works out cheaper in the end than going everywhere by taxi.

The city tours concentrate on just a few places, because Kyoto's chief sights, gardens, temples and shrines are far apart from one another. Kyoto has more than 1600 temples, and even a week's visit is too short for more than an impression of the city's richness. It is, however, without any doubt the most beautiful city in Japan, and a stay of just two or three days is enough to gain some idea of the splendour of old Japan.

The sights are too numerous to list here. It is only possible to provide a summary of some of the more unusual places which tourists should visit even if they are in Kyoto for only a short while.

Sanjusan-gen-do

E of the Main Railway Station stands Sanjusan-gen-do, the "Temple of the 33 Niches", which takes its name from the way it is built. Its façade is divided into 33 (sanjusan) niches (gen), to reflect the belief that Kannon, the goddess of compassion, could take on 33 different personifications.

The Temple was originally built in 1164. The present building was put up in 1266, after a fire. In days gone by archery competitions used to be held in the Temple grounds, as is still shown clearly by the holes in the pillars and timbers.

The most important work of art in the Temple is the "Kannon with a Thousand Hands". This statue, which is 10 ft (3·30 m) high, dates from the 13th c. On each side of it are 500 standing figures of Kannon.

In the passage behind it there are further sculptures – 28 "celestial auxiliaries", spirits who are subordinate to Kannon.

Nijo Palace

In the centre, opposite the International Hotel, stands the Nijo Palace, a complex covering 70 acres (28 ha) which is surrounded by walls and gates. The Palace was built in 1603 as the residence of the first Tokugawa Shogun, Ieyasu, when he was visiting the city. During the Meiji period it was first the seat of government, then the city hall.

Kyoto – the Imperial Seat until 1869 ▶

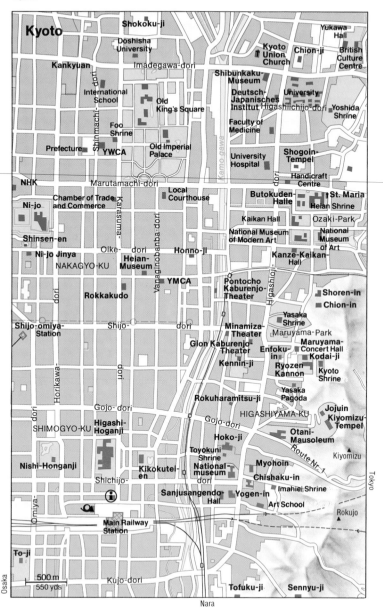

Kyoto

Entry to the Palace is through the E Gate, and visitors who take a guided tour then go through five huge palatial buildings interconnected by corridors the rooms of which possess almost unbelievable splendour. Shoes have to be removed as is customary when entering a Japanese residence. The floorboards in the corridors were laid in such a way as to squeak when walked on; the purpose was to prevent an enemy from slipping away unnoticed. The name of the corridors is "Nightingale Passages".

The "Ambassadors' Chamber" (1st building) and the "Audience Chamber of the Shoguns" (3rd building) are especially impressive. The decoration of their interior walls, dating from the early 17th c., is considered one of the best examples of Japanese interior architectural design. the Shogun had his private apartments in the 5th building. When their master was present there were always Samurai on guard in hidden little chambers off his living quarters, secretly keeping watch over him.

The Chion-in Temple, the main seat of the Jodo sects, is situated in the E of the city. It is one of Japan's most famous temples and its precinct covers 35 acres (14·5 ha). Its buildings, which were frequently destroyed by fire, were rebuilt for the last time at the beginning of the 17th c. Its 77 ft (24 m) high, two-storey tower, Sammon-san, is reputedly the most magnificent gate-tower in Japan, and its campanile houses the country's largest bell; it stands 18 ft (5·4 m) high, has a diameter of 9 ft (2·70 m), weighs 71 tons (74 tonnes), and was cast in 1633. It is rung only during the festivals which take place in mid-April.

Chion-in Temple

Nijo Palace in Kyoto

After the main hall, which is dedicated to Honen, the founder of the sect who lies buried here, and the assembly hall, the major attraction is the impressive Sutra Library. This houses a complete collection of the Buddhist Sutra, in 5600 volumes, which was printed in China at the time of the Sung Dynasty.

Kiyomizu Temple

The Kiyomizu Temple, which like the Chion-in Temple, is in the E part of the city, is situated on a hill up which runs a road known as "Tea-pot lane" (good porcelain). The Temple was founded in 790 and is dedicated to the eleven-headed Kannon. (The statue of her is a protected monument.) The present buildings were erected after 1633 in the period of the third Tokugawa Shogun, Iemitsu. They stand mainly on a rocky outcrop above the Otowa Waterfall. The terrace of the main hall makes a particularly strong impression. It rests on 95 ft (30 m) tall pillars with five rows of cross-beams. It is used as a stage for temple dances and ceremonies, and from it there is a wonderful view over the city. There is a Japanese saying which defines foolhardiness as jumping down from the terrace of Kiyomizu Temple.

Kinkakuji Temple

N of the city by a little lake stands the delightful Golden Pavilion (kinkakuji) which in 1955 was restored in the style of the original building, dating from 1397, which had been burnt down. The three storeys are of different periods. Their designs are, however, in perfect harmony. The roof is crowned by a bronze phoenix.
The pavilion takes its name from the gold leaf covering its exterior walls. As well as the statues of Kannon, etc., the mural paintings are particularly noteworthy.
In the park of this Buddhist temple complex – it belongs to the Rinzai sect – there is also a little teahouse.

Ryoanji Temple

The Ryoanji Temple stands in the N part of the city. It was founded in 1473 and belongs to the Rinzai sect. It is particularly worth a visit on account of its Zen stone garden which is renowned far beyond the confines of Kyoto as a place for meditation. The patterning created by the groups of rocks of various sizes is conducive to meditation of every kind. The rocks which are placed on smooth-raked expanses of ground could, for instance, be mountains emerging from the clouds, islands in the sea, or elements of a picture.

Daitokuji Temple

After the Kinkakuji and Ryoānji Temples the Daitokuji Temple is the most remarkable Buddhist temple complex in the N of the city.
It was founded in 1324 and is one of the chief temples of the Rinzai sect. Its present buildings date for the most part from the 16th and 17th c. Among its artistic treasures are paintings, Buddhist statues of the 15th and 16th c., old manuscript scrolls, wonderfully crafted portals and seven minor temples which all have their individual gardens.
The Daisen-in behind the main temple is rated the most important garden in this temple precinct, and indeed in all Zen Buddhism. It is in the Karesansui style and was laid out in the 16th c. The materials used – sand and pebbles – are so ingeniously placed that they give a picture of what they are supposed to represent – waterfalls, river, cranes, tortoises and treasure ship.

Kinkakuji Temple in Kyoto – the Golden Pavilion

Zen Stone Garden in Ryoanji Temple – rocks and white sand

Kyoto

Heian Shrine

The Heian Shrine, to the E of the city, was built in 1885 to mark the 1100th anniversary of the foundation of Kyoto. It was dedicated to the city's founder, Emperor Kammu (737–806), and to the last Emperor to reside there, Emperor Komei (1831–66).

The buildings are small-scale reproductions of the palace of the first Emperor. They are painted red and white, with blue roof tiles, and in this combination of colours the influence of China which is characteristic of the Heian period (794–1192) may be seen quite clearly.

The Shrine itself comprises two main halls, a state apartment, two towers and a large red-painted Torii made of reinforced concrete.

A large landscaped garden extends behind the Shrine.

Nanzenji Temple

As well as the Heian Shrine there is another temple worth visiting in the E of the city. It is the Nanzenji Temple which belongs to the Rinzai sect. (Other temple complexes belonging to this sect in the N are the Kinkajuji, Ryoanji and Daitokuji Temples.)

The Temple was founded in 1293. It is delightfully situated in the middle of a copse at the foot of a hill. Its most important attraction is its two-storey Torii, dating from 1628, with ceiling-paintings by famous contemporary artists. There are also panels on the sliding walls in the main hall. The portrayal of tigers in a bamboo thicket is particularly striking.

This temple complex, too, has a stone garden.

Heian Shrine in Kyoto

The Ginkakuji (or Silver Pavilion) Temple lies in the NE part of the city. In contrast to the Kinkakuji (or Golden Pavilion) Temple, this was never decorated with a covering of silver.

Ginkakuji Temple

It was built in 1482 by the eighth Ashikaga Shogun as a country residence. On his death it was converted into a Zen temple. It stands by a pool in which the two-storey building is reflected. In its upper storey it houses a gilded statue of Kannon. Behind it is the main hall with an important statue of Buddha. There is a tearoom adjacent.

There are two other rooms which are interesting. They are supposed to have been used as incense chambers. Just as Zen Buddhism created the Tea Ceremony (see Practical Information, Tea Ceremony) and Ikebana (see entry), in order to discipline the senses of taste and sight, it also made arrangements for occasions when people came together and incense was burnt in order to develop and improve the sense of smell.

Marunouchi (City District)

E/F 4/5

Marunouchi is the economic heart of Tokyo. It is here that nearly all the major banks and firms have their head offices in modern western-style high-rise blocks which have replaced the Samurai houses of yesteryear. Here stands Tokyo's Main Railway Station, modelled on Amsterdam's Central Station and built in red brick (E side) in 1914. In 1964 it acquired an addition for the Shinkansen Line (see entry). Each day there are 3000 train movements through this station. Nearby are to be

District
Chiyoda-ku

Underground Station
Nijubashi-mae

Marunouchi – the economic heart of Tokyo

found the offices of the Japanese National Railway (JNR), the Japan Travel Bureau (JTB, see Practical Information, Travel Agents) and the Head Post Office.

Marunouchi is also the political centre of Tokyo. It is here that the Tenno lives in the Imperial Palace (see entry) with its surrounding wall. S of the Palace walls lies the government district, with the Parliament Building (see entry) and the ministries. Tokyo's City Hall (see entry) is just a few minutes away from the Main Railway Station. Last, but not least, Marunouchi is also a shopping centre, with the Daimaru store (see Practical Information, Stores) and a range of underground shops.

Culturally Marunouchi is remarkable for its sacred buildings (see entries for Yasukuni Shrine and Hie Shrine), a number of museums (Museum of Science, National Museum of Modern Art, see Practical Information, Museums), theatres (Music Hall and National Theatre, see Practical Information, Theatres) and the National Library (Kokkai-toshokan).

Meiji Shrine B5

District
Shibuya-ku

Railway Station
Harajuku (Yamanote Line)

Underground Station
Meiji-jingumae
(Chiyoda Line)

The Meiji Shrine is one of the most popular Shinto places of worship in Tokyo. It was founded in 1920, destroyed during the war and restored in traditional style. It is dedicated to the Emperor Meiji (1868–1912). He it was who put an end to the 600-year-long rule of the Shoguns and led Japan into the modern era. Around the Shrine stretches the 180 acre (72 ha) Inner Garden.

The Main Torii is impressive. 40 ft (13 m) high, it is Japan's

Torii in the Park in front of the Meiji Shrine

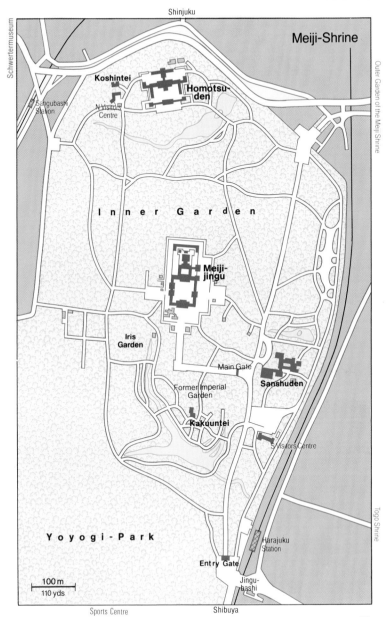

Meiji-Shrine

Shinjuku

Schwertermuseum

Outer Garden of the Meiji Shrine

Koshintei

Homotsu-den

Sangubashi Station

N Visitors Centre

Inner Garden

Meiji-jingu

Iris Garden

Main Gate

Sanshuden

Former Imperial Garden

Kakuuntei

S Visitors Centre

Yoyogi-Park

Togo Shrine

Harajuku Station

100 m
110 yds

Entry Gate

Jingu-bashi

Sports Centre

Shibuya

Meiji Shrine

Iris Garden at the Meiji Shrine

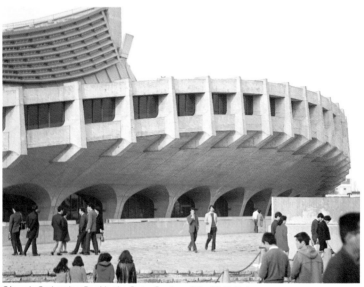

Olympic Swimming Pool in the Outer Garden of the Meiji Shrine

tallest wooden gate, made of ancient Hinoki tree-trunks from Taiwan. Gravel pathways lead to the sanctuary with its hall for devotions and its main hall. The faithful pour water over their hands and symbolically cleanse their mouths at a fountain by the entrance, as religious custom requires. Furthermore, they remove their hats and coats before entering the Shrine.

A little to one side lies the Treasury. There artistic and ritual objects once belonging to Meiji-tenno are conserved. They illustrate the outlook on life of the period.

In the S of the Park lies the Iris Garden. At the end of June and the beginning of July its flowers bloom with almost unbelievable magnificence.

The most important festivals are the birthday of Meijo-tenno (3 November) and the Celebration of Spring (29 April–3 May), with performances of the old Bugaku court music and tourneys. There is an archery competition for horsemen, sometimes clad as Samurai, who ride galloping steeds. At New Year there is a display of the most expensive Kimonos at the Meiji Shrine, but the crowds are enormous.

Opening times
daily 9 a.m.–4 p.m.

Outer Garden of the Meiji Shrine
with the Yoyogi Sports Centre and Memorial Picture Gallery

The Outer Garden of the Meiji Shrine is connected with the Inner Garden by an expressway. In this precinct are to be found the Crown Prince's Palace (see entry for Akasaka Palace), the Yoyogi Sports Centre and the Memorial Picture Gallery.

The Yoyogi Sports Centre was built for the Summer Olympic Games in 1964. It comprises a swimming-pool, a Budokan hall and the National Stadium. The vast swimming pool building was designed by Japan's most famous architect, Tange Kenzo, and cost more than six million dollars (about £4,000,000). It is still used for swimming, but an ice-rink has been added. On occasions everything is cleared away for an international tennis tournament. The swimming pool's roof is suspended on steel cables which are anchored in two rocks. The Budokan Hall, not far from the Imperial Palace (see entry) was designed for martial sports, such as Judo (see entry). Nowadays it is also used on various occasions for celebrations.

The National Stadium is in Meiji Park. It was orginally put up for the Asiatic Games in 1958 and then enlarged for the Olympics. 80,000 spectators can watch football matches and athletic competitions here.

Location
Shibuya

Railway Station
Harajuku

The Memorial Picture Gallery is in the N part of the Park. It was opened in 1925. Its exhibits come from the period of Meiji-tenno's reign.

Memorial Picture Gallery

Metropolitan Fine Art Gallery of Tokyo   F2

The Tokyo Metropolitan Fine Art Gallery has on show works by modern Japanese painters. Throughout the year there are also temporary exhibitions.

The Gallery is open daily (except Mons.) from 9 a.m. to 4 p.m. Those interested in art should, however, also visit the exhibitions in the stores and galleries which normally maintain a comparable standard.

Underground Station
Ueno-ku (Ginza Line)

Railway Station
Ueno

Museum of General Communications F4

Location
2-1-4, Otemachi,
Chiyoda-ku

Railway Station
Main Railway Station

Opening times
daily (except Mon.)
9 a.m.–4.30 p.m.

The General Communications Museum is just five minutes' walk from the Main Railway Station. It is a veritable Aladdin's Cave for philatelists. Every collector will be enthralled by its collection of postage stamps in which Japan and the Asiatic area are particularly well represented.

All those who are interested in the techniques of communication will also find a great deal here. The Museum has on show a complete collection of documents illustrating the history of Japanese postal and telecommunication techniques.

**National Museum of Tokyo F2

Location
Ueno Park, Taito-ku

Railway Station
Ueno (Yamanote Line)

Opening times
daily, except Mon.
9 a.m.–4 p.m.

Closed
26 Dec.–3 Jan.

The National Museum of Tokyo houses more than 100,000 works of Japanese, Chinese and Indian art, including more than 100 of Japan's National Treasures. Its main building comprises 25 exhibition galleries (of which 20 are normally open to the public). It was built between 1932 and 1938 to replace the Imperial Museum, which was seriously damaged in the 1923 earthquake, and presented to the Imperial House. The latter ceded all proprietary rights over the building and its artistic treasures to the state in 1947. Until 1868 the Kan-eiji Temple stood here; it was at the time the most important Buddhist temple in Edo. In 1875 the temple was rebuilt close by, just outside the park.

On the right hand side of the main building lies the Museum for E Asiatic Art, with 15 exhibition galleries. It was opened in October 1968. The objects on display are changed from time to time.

Rooms 1–3: Buddhist sculptures from the Asuka Period (552–645) to the present, as well as examples from China.

Room 4: Old textiles, especially valuable examples from the Asuka Period.

Room 5: Metalwork, especially Buddhist sacred vessels, etc. (6th–16th c.).

Room 6: Historical weapons and military equipment.

Room 7: The art of the swordsmith is illustrated with exhibits from different centuries.

Room 8: Historic Japanese clothing. Ceramics from Japan, China and Korea.

Rooms 9 and 10: Japanese, Korean and Chinese pottery from various periods.

Room 11: Japanese painting from the Nara Period (645–794) to the Kamakura Period (1192–1336).

Room 12: Japanese painting from the Muromachi Period (1392–1573) including masterpieces by the monks, Josetsu, Shubun and Sesshu.

General impression of the Tokyo National Museum

Room 13: Japanese painting from the Momoyama (1573–1603) and Tokugawa (1603–1868) periods, including works of the Kano, Tosa, Sumiyoshi, Korin and Maruyama schools.

Room 14: Coloured xylographs from the Tokugawa Period.

Rooms 15 and 16: Japanese and Chinese masterpieces of lacquer-work of various centuries, including examples of lacquer-carving, gold lacquer, lacquer with mother of pearl, etc.

Rooms 17 and 18: Japanese painting of the Meiji Period.

Rooms 19 and 20: Masterpieces of Japanese calligraphy; examples from the Nara Period to the Tokugawa Period.

A suggestion: the Museum has excellent coloured postcards with impressive reproductions of the most important exhibits.

There are two other galleries near the main building:
Hyokeikan: objects excavated from graves, settlements, etc., reveal the prehistory of Japan. The so-called Haniwa, pottery figures which were buried with the dead, are especially worthy of note.
Toyokan: objects from China and Korea.

Hyokeikan, Toyokan

Behind the main building there is a typical Japanese landscape garden. Three pavilions have been brought here, and they give it the character of an open-air museum. The Tein Teahouse

Landscaped Garden

National Museum of Western Art

(Rokuso-an) dates from the 17th c. In the Okyo Pavilion (Okyo-kan) pictures with plant motives by the famous landscape artist Maruyama Okyo (1735–95) are on show, while pictures by Kano School painters are displayed in the Kujo Pavilion. There is also a storehouse from the Kamakura Period.

Suggestion

Horyuji-homotsukan, the Treasure of the Horyuji Temple near Nara which was completed in 1964, lies nearby. It is, however, open only on Thursdays when the weather is good.

National Museum of Western Art   F2

Location
Ueno Park, Taito-ku

Railway Station
Ueno (Yamanote Line)

Opening times
daily (except Mon.)
9.30 a.m.–4.30 p.m.

The National Museum of Western Art is to be found in Ueno Park (see entry) just three minutes' walk from Ueno Station. It was built in 1959, to plans by the famous Swiss architect Le Corbusier. The exhibits – works of French artists for the most part – come mainly from the collection made by Kojiro Matsukata during his visit to Europe early in the present century.

In the courtyard works by the French sculptor Auguste Rodin are on show, together with canvases by the Impressionists Paul Cézanne, Claude Monet, Edouard Manet and Edgar Degas.

Visitors who have already visited the great art collections in either the capital cities of Europe or in the United States will not need to visit this exhibition of Western art in Tokyo. they will be disappointed, for masterpieces are not represented here.

National Science Museum   F2

Location
Ueno Park, Taito-ku

Underground Station
Ueno-eki (Ginza Line)

Railway Station
Ueno (Yamanote Line)

Just a few minutes' walk from Ueno Station in the E part of Ueno Park (see entry) can be found the National Science Museum. There are departments for space research, atomic research, applied chemistry, architecture, electricity and transport, etc. as well as a laboratory and a work room.

The Museum is open every day (except Mon.) from 9.30 a.m. to 4.30 p.m.

**Nikko

Railway
From Asakusa (Tobu Line)
by private railway to Tobu
Nikko

Location
93 miles (150 km) N

The little township of Nikko with around 50,000 inhabitants, lies some 93 miles (150 km) N of Tokyo. No visitor interested in Japanese culture should be put off by the distance. Nikko – which is well supplied with antique shops – is famous for its shrines, its national park and its wonderful setting where lakes alternate with wooded knolls, rivers and thermal springs. The highest waterfall in Japan is to be found here, too. In Japan some 60,000 monkeys live in the wild, and some of them can be seen here. Visitors wishing to make the journey by railway can travel by several different routes; The quickest ($1\frac{3}{4}$ hours journey time) is from Asakusa underground station (ask to be directed to the Nikko Line of the Tobu Railway, the ticket office of which is in the same building). Japanese National Railway trains leave from Ueno Station and the journey by express takes about 2 hours.

Nikko – a township in a lovely setting ▶

Nikko

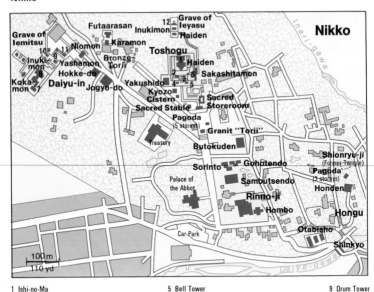

1 Ishi-no-Ma
2 Mikoshigura
3 Yomeimon
4 Drum Tower

5 Bell Tower
6 Kaguraden
7 Honden
8 Haiden

9 Drum Tower
10 Bell Tower
11 Nitemmon
12 Hote

The Japan Travel Bureau (see Practical Information, Travel Agents) also organises day excursions to Nikko; an afternoon bus tour around the National Park is included in the price.

Visitors who make their own way to Nikko should walk across the township's only main street and go uphill from the railway station for a quarter of an hour until they come to the Sacred Bridge. This red-lacquered structure with an elegant curve spans the Daiya River. It is now open only during festivals. Close-by is the modern bridge for everyday use. Beyond it lie the temple precincts, with the Rinnoji Temple, the Toshogu Shrine and the Daiyuinbyo Mausoleum of Iemitsu.

Rinnoji Temple

The Rinnoji Temple was founded in 766 and belongs to the Tendai Sect. With a main hall 125 ft (38 m) long and 93 ft (28 m) high, it is reckoned to be the largest building in Nikko. The interior is dominated by three gigantic statues, and Amida Buddha, and two of Kannon, the goddess of mercy, portrayed in one instance with a thousand arms.

S of this Temple stands the 43 ft (13 m) high Sorinto bronze pillar. On it are the 10,000 sacred maxims, the so-called "Sutras" or "Guiding Threads".

The Toshogu Shrine is the most important religious building in Nikko. It dates from 1634–6 and is dedicated to Ieyasu (1542–1616), the founder of the Tokugawa Shogunate. All the buildings, with the exception of the Sacred Stable, are lacquered red and embellished with metal leaf.

Rinnoji Temple – Kannon with a thousand arms and Amida Buddha

The Three Sacred Monkeys of Nikko – hear no evil, speak no evil, see no evil

There are signs indicating the way steeply uphill to this temple complex. At its entry stands the five-storey Go-ju-no-to Pagoda which was constructed in 1815. Visitors enter through the Nio-mon Gate (Gate of the Heavenly Kings), and pass the Holy Stable in the carvings of which are portrayed the celebrated Wise Monkeys of Nikko who cover their ears, mouth and eyes with their paws, hearing nothing, saying nothing and seeing nothing (photograph, p. 73). The Sacred Granary is seen next, with its remarkable elephant relief on the top. Visitors then go through a second gate which leads into the Middle Courtyard.

The path then leads through the Yomeimon Gate ("Gate of Sunlight", which is also sometimes called the "Twilight Gate"). This is reputedly the finest gate in all Japan. Finally entry into the Shrine is through the Karamon (Chinese) Gate. The Shrine itself is divided into the Prayer Hall and the main hall (Honden). On its N side is found the bronze funerary monument of Ieyasu.

E of the Toshogu Shrine stands another shrine, the Futaarsan Shrine, and the Shihonryuji Temple.

A guided tour of the Shrines here takes around three hours.

The Daiyuninbyo Mausoleum is situated W of the Toshogu Shrine. It is the funerary monument ot Ieyasu's grandson Iemitsu. In its layout, with gates, courtyards, main shrine and grave, it is very similar to the Toshogu Shrine.

Chugushi Shrine

Visitors who have the time and energy should also go to see the Chugushi Shrine on the shore of Lake Chuzenji. It belongs to the Futa-arasan Shrine. It may be reached from the station in about 40 minutes either by bus or taxi. The journey offers an opportunity of appreciating the beauty of the countryside at Nikko.

Nikko: Boating on Lake Chezenji

Noh: classic Japanese Theatre

Noh

With its courtly ritual restraint and reflecting the Samurai spirit in the suppression of feelings Noh theatre generally does not mean much to foreigners. For it is in almost everything the opposite of Kabuki (see entry). The stage is dominated by the costumes and masks. Heroes and divine powers are supposed to evoke wonder. And the mysticism with its roots in religion cannot be overlooked. Just one syllable stressed in a certain way or a slight movement of the hand reveals to the cognoscenti the drama which is going on. But all this means nothing to those who have not been told the story beforehand. Drum, flute and chorus accompany the story just as they were formerly used at the incantation of spells. Noh actors wear masks particularly in the main roles. These masks are in themselves works of art and of incalculable value if they have the patina of age.

Noh is in fact regarded by many Japanese less as a sort of theatre than as an attitude towards life or a philosophy as an abstraction of dreams, thoughts and life which can hardly be comprehended.

To find out where and when Noh performances take place see Practical Information, Theatre and Information.

Performances
Ginza Noh Theatre
Kanze Noh Theatre
Kita Noh Theatre
National Theatre

Oshima (island)

Oshima (the Big Island) lies 72 miles (117 km) from Tokyo. By ship it takes 4 hours to get there, but by plane it is only half an

Ship
From Takashiba Quay

Pachinko

Flights
From Hanada

Location
72 miles (117 km) S

hour. Thermal springs near Yuba and blooming fields of camellias and camellia bushes for which the island is famous, show Japanese nature in all its beauty. They bloom during the months of winter and are the raw material for making hair oil. The island is a favourite resort for Tokyo's inhabitants. The chief attraction is the volcano Mihira whose last major eruptions were in 1942 and 1951. Visitors who care to can easily climb to the top (by bus to Gojinkachaya, then 322 steps). At the summit there is generally some mist and crowds of tourists. Suggestion: when female visitors buy a typical headscarf with camellia blossoms, they will also be loaned a blue and white kimono which completes the island costume and they can then be photograhed as "ankosan" or "shima" girls.

Pachinko

Visitors who are fascinated by pin-ball tables at home should not fail to venture into a Pachinko gallery. Little steel balls dance on flimsy pillars and, if they fall into the right hole, bring the reward in the shape of more little steel balls as lights flash and bells ring out. Every third Japanese sits for a few hours a week playing his favourite game of chance and skill, and at the end he can exchange his winnings (if any!) for olive oil, cigarettes and stockings for his wife. Anybody who goes into a pin-ball gallery where hundreds of Pachinko fans sit around at every hour of the day or night receives a friendly welcome and is given an explanation about the tricks a beginner needs to know. There is no need to speak the language either, because the visitor from abroad has already demonstrated that he is a true friend of Japan. It is not expensive either: 35 balls cost only 150 yen (in 1981).

* Paper Museum

Location
1-1-8 Horifune, Kita-ku

Railway Station
Oji

Opening times
daily (except Mon.)
9.30 a.m.–4.30 p.m.

In Japan paper is rated as a variety of art, and out in the country it is still possible to see how it is made.

The Tokyo Paper Museum is the only one of its type in the world. It has a rich display of various kinds of paper and, above all, prints. Also on show is the equipment needed for making paper by hand.

Visitors who wish to take back home printed paper as a souvenir can purchase enchanting examples in many shops and particularly in the Tokyo Hands Store in Shibuya (see Practical Information, Stores).

Park for Nature Study   C/D7

Underground Station
Meguro (Yamanote Line)

The Park for Nature Study, which lies 10 minutes' walk from Meguro Underground Station, is somewhat gloomy in appearance because of its many laurel-type trees. It is not a park for the people, like Ueno Park (see entry), nor a park with traditional Japanese landscape architecture, like Shinjuku Park (see entry). Rather it is a collection of plants with special significance. Many groups of students walk around it with their teacher, to observe the birds, insects and vegetation. The park always closes early according to the time of year.

Parliament Building (Kokkai-Gijido)   E5

The Parliament Building, also referred to as the "National Diet Building", stands in the government district of Marunouchi (see entry). In Japanese it is called Kokkai-Gijido. A form of government which has been taken over from the West can only be represented in a building which has no connection with Japanese architectural styles.

The vast, massive grey-granite building is modelled on the American Congress. It has a portico supported on columns and a central tower 200 ft (65 m) high which is also colonnaded and surmounted by a stepped pyramid. The pompous hideousness of this structure which was completed in 1936 recalls the architecture of the Nazi period in Germany.

But the Japanese are fast learners, and just as they gave democracy a typical Japanese stamp so, too, they have tried to link western architectural styles tastefully with the Japanese character.

The right-hand wing of the building is for the Upper House. In the left-hand wing the Lower House meets (see Introduction, Japan's Government). In the entrance hall stand bronzes of the "fathers of Japanese parliamentarism" – Prince Ito, Okum and Itagaki.

District
Marunouchi

Underground Station
Kokkai-Gijido-mae

Parliament

*Rikugien Park   E1

District
Bunkyo-ku

Railway Station
Komagome (Yamanote Line)

Opening times
daily (except Mon.)
9 a.m.–4.30 p.m.

This entrancingly beautiful park is only eight minutes' walk from the Railway Station. It is a characteristic example of 18th c. landscaping, with a knoll, called Tsukiyama, a lake and an island. What is unusual is the fact that the various landscape features are all connected with literary themes. The park was laid out for a counsellor of the Tokugawa Shogunate. Since 1938 it has been in the ownership of the City of Tokyo. Nearby is the Gokokuji Temple (see entry).

Ryokan

A Ryokan is a traditional Japanese inn, and as such is equipped for the requirements and way of life of the inhabitants of the country. Yet to a certain extent it is possible for a tourist from the west to experience here everyday, Japanese life.

It is advisable to note down in Japanese script the name and address of the selected Ryokan (if necessary with the help of a tourist office) and to show this address to the taxi driver. On arrival you should keep the taxi waiting until you are absolutely certain of being at the correct address. You push back the gate, enter the doorway and step in to the lower level of the hallway but you do not proceed to the upper level. Here you are greeted with much bowing and smiling and it is a rule of politeness to reciprocate. Then you take off your outdoor shoes and proceed

Ryokan – the traditional Japanese guest house

to the upper level. Here slippers are provided which must be worn inside the house; the rooms which are laid out with tatami (rush mats) may only be entered wearing socks or stockings. Other shoes are provided when you wish to visit the toilet. Many Ryokans only have the kind of toilets customary in Japan and these are similar to those in certain countries in southern Europe. For Europeans, who are not accustomed to them, the necessary squatting can be rather uncomfortable.

Indoor clothing is also provided; a light yukata (indoor kimono), which can also serve as a garment for sleeping, and worn over it the heavy "tanzen", the broad sleeves of which also serve as pockets. At night the maid lays out the bed on the floor. It consists of a thin quilted mattress and a small pillow filled with rice. In the morning the bedding is put back into a cupboard.

Normally in a Ryokan two meals, breakfast and supper, are served daily; both are included in the price of the room; Japanese cuisine is customary.

Bathing in the Ryokan, called "O-furo", is one of the delights of Japanese life (but more of a torture for the uninitiated!). It is advisable for a European to take his bath last, for then the water is no longer as boiling hot as the Japanese like it. The maid is told that you wish to bath (the word "O-furo" is sufficient) and she puts your name on the list (more expensive rooms are provided with a private bathroom). You soap yourself thoroughly and carefully rinse off all the soapsuds before you get into the hot bath water. The bath tub is for pleasure and not for cleansing; the hot water remains in the bath for the user!

In the whole of Japan there are about 70,000 Ryokans. About

Sengakuji Temple – stone memorials to the 47 Ronins

2000 of these are furnished according to official standards, so that, as far as board and lodging and sanitary arrangements are concerned, they equate with European practice. The others are usually also very good, but wholly geared to Japanese guests and without staff speaking foreign languages.

**Sengakuji Temple   D7

Location
Takanawa

Underground
Sengakuji (Toei–Asakusa Line)

Railway Station
Sinagawa

Even today the fate of the 47 Samurai who avenged the death of their master is still lamented, especially by women. In the 18th c. their fate moved the minds of all the Japanese. They all lie buried in the Sengakuji Temple. The faithful still come every day to light joss sticks to their memory on their stone memorials in the beautiful temple gardens.

Their lord and master, Asano Naganoni, Lord of Ako (1659–1703) drew his sword when the court chamberlain Kira Yoshinaka insulted and wounded him. This action, on Imperial ground, was rated as a crime which could be atoned only by death, and the Daimyo was accordingly sentenced to commit "Seppuku" (ritual suicide).

His Samurai, who now had no master any longer and were deprived of his protection, became "ronin" (i.e. men of the waves); they had no longer a home and their lives were purposeless. They had no desire, moreover, to enter the service of any other Daimyo. Instead their desire was to avenge their master; in accord with the code of honour of the Samurai, that was an action proving the noblest sort of devotion.

For months on end they adopted an air of indifference, made a show of being reconciled to events and prepared slowly for the day of reckoning: Kira was to be slain and, as a sign of propitiation and satisfaction, his head was to be placed on their master's grave which was in the Sengakuji Temple.

And so it came to pass. Led by Oishi Yoshio, also known as Oishi Kuranosuke, they burst into Kira's lodging and struck off his head. This they cleaned and then placed on the grave stone. This deed was recognised as highly meritorious. But the Samurai were obliged, like their master, to die by their own hand. With the satisfaction of having served their master loyally even after his death and of having restored his honour, they did as they were sentenced to do not far from Asano's grave.

Their heroic deeds are immortalised as a symbol of loyalty in the Kabuki play "Chushingura".

The graves of the 47 Ronins are in the Temple Cemetery. The Temple itself was founded in 1612 by the Zen Buddhist Soto Sect. The main temple building is a reconstruction, dating from 1953. The Main Gate – Sammon – dates back to the mid 19th c.

Shinjuku (District of Tokyo)   B/C 3/4

District
Shinjuku-ku

Underground
Shinjuku (Marunouchi Line)

Railway Station
Shinjuku (Chuo and Yamanote Lines)

Shinjuku forms the W part of Tokyo. It is a secondary centre of population and trade situated some 7 miles (10 km) from the centre of the capital. During the Edo period (1603–1867) Naito-Shinjuku was a posting station. Nowadays it is one of the busiest traffic junctions in Tokyo. Shinjuku Station, serving railway and underground, handles vast numbers of commuters each day.

E of the Railway Station stands the second-largest shopping

centre in Tokyo (see Practical Information, Shopping Centres), with stores and an underground mall. Above all, here is to be found the well-known entertainment district of Kabuki-cho with gaming dens, bars, cafés, jazz cellars, discos, cinemas, theatres and galleries.

There are also several skyscrapers which at one time were something of a rarity in Japan. Among them are the Keio Plaza Intercontinental Hotel (558 ft (169 m) and 47 storeys), the Shinjuku-Sumitono Building (660 ft (200 m) and 52 storeys), the Shinjuku-Mitsui Building (640 ft (212 m) and 55 storeys). From the viewing platforms at the top of the skyscrapers there is a magnificent view over the city at night time.

The Shinjuku Park (see entry) and the Waseda University with its Tsubouchi Theatre Museum (see entry) are to be found in Shinjuku.

Shinjuku Park (Shinjuku-gyoen)   C4

Japanese garden design, with what strikes foreigners as a completely different style of artistic arrangement, is an unfailing source of delight. The Shinjuku-Gyoen National Garden is a park that combines everything which is expected of Japanese gardening. It is situated only five minutes' walk from Shinjuku Railway Station.

The grounds of the Park cover some 145 acres (58·5 ha). Formerly most of it belonged to the Naito family of Daimyos. Towards the end of the 19th c. it came into the possession of the Imperial house which transferred ownership to the state after the Second World War.

District
Shinjuku-ku

Underground Station
Shinjuku-gyoen-mae
(Marunouchi Line)

Opening times
daily (except Mon.)
9 a.m.–4 p.m.

Closed
29 Dec.–3 Jan.

Skyscrapers in Shinjuku

Shinkansen Super Express

As the Park is also a botanical garden, with botanical specimens from all over the world, it is divided into two main sections, one European and the other Japanese. The models for the European section were the French parks and the English landscaped garden. The Japanese section, with its pretty pavilion in the Chinese style, attracts crowds of visitors, particularly in April when the cherry trees are covered in blossom. At that time of the year 1100 trees comprising 34 different varieties may be seen in all their glory. Those who prefer chrysanthemums wait for November when chrysanthemum shows are held in the Park.

*Shinkansen

Reservations
Japan Travel Bureau

Tall tourists who fancy a long journey by the fastest trains in the world are well advised to book seats in the so-called "green cars" (first class), because even the Shinkansen is designed for average Japanese. Nevertheless, the journey from Tokyo to Fukuoka – that is 735 miles (1176 km) – is accomplished in just seven hours. Service on the train is first rate. Snacks of every sort, including Japanese o-bento, are always available, and the Shinkansen travels so smoothly that it is also possible to sleep peacefully. Another reason why passengers can be relaxed is because there is an automatic warning system to ensure that the train will stop if a typhoon blows up or if there is an earthquake, or else it will be diverted into a specially constructed shelter.

The Shinkansen is Japan's most important transport system,

In the Shinkansen

because along the N–S axis there is, apart from this, only one expressway and this is generally jammed with traffic. Tickets, which are also seat reservations, should be bought as far as possible before the date of travelling; this is especially important when travelling on Japanese holidays. On such days millions of tourists are on the move, for they generally have only a short regular holiday.

The Shinkansen Line links Tokyo with Nagoya, Kyoto, Osaka, Kobe, Okayama, Hiroshima, Kitakyushu and Fukuoka. The line also goes N to Sendai and Morioka. Other Shinkansen lines are under construction to Niigata and Narita, and an extension from Morioka to Aomori and eventually to Sapporo is planned. There are two types of train plying on the route: the "Hikari" (Light or Lightning) which stops only at the major cities and reaches a speed of almost 125 mph (200 km/h), and the "Kodama" (Echo) which takes appreciably longer because it stops at the less important stations.

It is best to obtain tickets either from hotels or from the Japan Travel Bureau (see Practical Information, Travel Agents). Information about seat availability is immediately available thanks to a comprehensive computer system.

Sumida River Trips

There are trips every day (except Tues.) on the Sumida, Tokyo's largest river. It may be true that the Sumida is no longer as delightful as the Seine, a claim which used to be made in days gone by. All the same, a trip on the river still is well worth while.

Trips
daily (except Tues.)

Far more of the city is seen from the river than is possible from any journey by underground railway.

A suggestion: it is best in any case to travel from the city centre to Asakusa (see entry), a city district which should on no account be missed.

The hotel provides information about where and at what time the trips begin.

*Sumo

Where to see it
Kuramae Kokugikan 2-1-9,
Kuramae, Taito-ku

Japanese wrestling is quite unlike the sport practised in western countries. A pair of heavyweights, often weighing as much as 24 stone, try, after all kinds of colourful preliminaries, including the rhythmic raising and slapping of their thighs, to force one another out of the ring, with heaves, tripping, and high throws. The bout can be finished in two seconds if one of the giants misses his grip and falls on his belly. It can also last for minutes, at the end of which the nervous tension is tremendous.

Two teams ("armies") fight one another in a sort of knock-out system. The victors win money and cups, which in their way are equally valuable, and above all they win the respect of their team, which means a great deal.

Any Japanese who can afford to do so comes to see these bouts in the arena; the rest of the nation sits watching them on TV.

Sumo wrestlers are destined to have only a short lifespan because their bodies are so heavy; they start putting on weight at a very early age. In the Middle Ages the bouts were a matter of life and death. Nowadays, however, a bout depends on which of the opponents is the first to touch the ground, whether within or outside the ring which is some 50 ft (15 m) across.

Women are never permitted to enter the ring; their presence would defile it.

Visitors to Tokyo should not miss any opportunity to see the Sumo tournaments. These take place three times a year in Tokyo, for a fortnight on each occasion in January, May and September.

Kuramae Kokugikan

The Sumo contests take place in Kuramae Kokugikan, which is also the headquarters of the Sumo Association. The 4-storey ferro-concrete building seats over 13,000 spectators.

Sumo Museum

The Sumo Museum is to be found near the entrance to Kuramae Kokugikan. On show are some 5000 Sumo-nishiki, that is woodcuts and photographs of famous Sumo wrestlers. It is open Mon.–Fri. from 9.30 a.m. to 4.30 p.m. and is closed on national holidays and in the period from 29 December to 4 January.

Tea Ceremony (Sa-do)

Displays
Hotel Okura, Imperial Hotel,
Hotel New Otani, Tea Room
of Suntory, Museum of Art,
Tea Room of Yamatane
Museum of Art

Tea appears on every occasion – at the beginning of a conversation, at the end of a meal, and, in an almost sacred rite, in the tea ceremony.

O-cha is the green tea found commonly everywhere. It is drunk without sugar from a cup without a handle. In restaurants it is

Tea Ceremony

served free at meals. In the tea ceremony, however, powdered tea is used.

The tea ceremony was originally introduced from China. It has a hygienic and a religious significance. Its philosophy was derived from Zen Buddhism in the 12th c. (see General, Population and Religion). Supporting Zen meditation its complex ritual is said to help the inner essence of objects to crystallise out, conveying their characteristic nature and developing the meaning which is inherent even in everday actions.

In earlier times the tea ceremony was practised in a separate tea pavilion some distance from the house and hidden in a garden setting. Nowadays, following ancient practice, beautiful pottery is used.

At the tea ceremony a group of silent people form a circle. The tea is ground down to a fine powder and stirred with a bamboo whisk until it foams. Every gesture has its meaning: the way the water is poured out, the tea whipped, the bowls held, examined and finally conveyed to the lips.

This ritual can be observed in many temples, and it is also possible, on payment of a small fee, to participate. Just as with Ikebana (see entry) there are various schools where the tea ceremony can be learned (see Practical Information, Cultural Events), and recognised tea masters. Every year millions of pupils, especially women register to learn the tea ceremony.

Tokyo Disneyland © *1983 Walt Disney Productions*

Tokyo Disneyland

Location
1 Maihama
Urayasu-shi
Chiba-ken 272–01

Telephone
54–2511

Road
Expressway No. 9
6 miles (10 km) from
city centre

Underground Station
Urayasu (Tozai line)

World Bazaar

Tokyo Disneyland, opened in April 1983, has behind it the proven expertise of more than 28 years of Disney experience in the theme park industry. Many of the most popular Disneyland attractions and restaurants found in the USA are incorporated into the Tokyo project, as well as several entirely new attractions, such as "Pinocchio's Daring Journey", "The Eternal Seas" and "Meet the World". In addition, there are up to 300 entertainers appearing daily in stage shows, musical performances and parades; and, of course, Mickey Mouse and all the other Disney characters can be found greeting visitors and signing autographs. There are more than 27 places to eat, ranging from snack bars to elaborate gourmet restaurants.

In contrast to "Main Street USA" of Disneyland and Walt Disney World, Tokyo Disneyland has a "World Bazaar", which is totally under cover and fully protected from the weather. It features a main street, courtyards, shops, boutiques, restaurants and entertainment – all reminiscent of America at the turn of the century. Visitors will pass through the World Bazaar on their way to other attractions: Adventureland, Fantasyland, Tomorrowland and Westernland.

Tokyo Tower ▶

*Tokyo Tower   E6

District
Minato-ku

Location
Shiba Park

Underground Station
Hamiyacho (Hibiya Line)

Railway Station
Hamamatsucho (Keihin-
Tohoku Line; Yamanote
Line)

On a hill in Shiba Park, where the Zojoji Temple (see entry) is also situated, stands Tokyo's tallest building. Tokyo Tower, which dates from 1958 and is modelled on the Eiffel Tower in Paris, is 1098 ft (333 m) high, 43 ft (13 m) taller than its Parisian predecessor. When visibility is good, visitors can even make out Fuji-san and there is always a good view over the gigantic city of Tokyo. There are viewing platforms at altitudes of 490 ft (150 m) and 795 ft (250 m).

Every year four million visitors climb or are conveyed to the top of this tower, which weighs some 4000 tons. The tower is both a symbol of Japanese post-war reconstruction and also a landmark for the city. It houses an aquarium with over 8000 species of fish, as well as the first waxworks in Asia. At its base stands the Museum of Modern Science.

Seven television stations and a host of radio transmitters make use of the tower which is also the transmission mast for radio communication between important undertakings. A battery of instruments constantly measures the amount of pollution over Tokyo. Seismatic indicators monitor the faintest earth tremors. The Japanese are extremely fond of eating and drinking, and the Tokyo Tower naturally contains several restaurants and cafés.

Tsubouchi Theatre Museum   C3

Location
1-chome, Nishi-Waseda
Shinjuku-ku

Underground Station
Waseda (Tozai Line)

Opening times
daily (except Mon.)
9 a.m.–4 p.m.

The grounds of Waseda University are five minutes' walk from Waseda Underground Station. The University was founded in 1882 by the politician Okuma Shigenobu (1838–1922). It is one of the country's largest institutions of higher education, with seven faculties in all.

The Tsubouchi Memorial Theatre Museum is situated on the campus. It was set up in 1928 as a memorial to Dr Tsubouchi Shoyo (1859–1935), a famous dramatist and translator of Shakespeare. It is the only museum of its type in Japan. Objects and documents are on show which illustrate the history and the nature of Far Eastern theatre. For those who are going to see Noh (see entry) and Kabuki (see entry) theatre, this is a very good source of additional information about a quite alien theatrical world.

*Tsukiji Fishmarket   F6

Railway Station
Shimbashi
(Yamanote–Ginza–Hibiya
Line)

In Japan much fish is eaten. But where does it come from? Much of it is imported. But whether deep-frozen or freshly caught, together with oysters, crayfish, ink-fish and crabs, all this mouth-watering food ends up by being displayed on Tokyo's famous fishmarket.

The market covers an area of 50 acres (20 ha). It lies 210 yd (200 m) S of the Tsukiji-Honganji Temple. Sales on this wholesale market commence at four in the morning every day. Accordingly it is best to visit the market between 4.30 a.m and

8 p.m. Wear watertight shoes and don't forget to take a spare film for your camera.

Tsukiji-Honganji Temple   F5

SE of the shopping street of Ginza (see entry) 320 yd (300 m) E of the Kabuki-za Temple stands the Tsukiji-Honganji Temple of the Jodo-Shinshu sect. It was founded in 1630 and is built in the Hindu style. It has been destroyed by fire several times, most recently at the time of the 1923 earthquake. The latest reconstruction dates from 1935.

It is noteworthy because weddings take place here, contrary to the practice of other Buddhist sects, and because there are Buddhist services in English on Sundays.

Location
Shin-ohashi-dori, Ginza

Railway Station
Yurakucho (Yamanote Line)

Tsukudajima (Island)

Thirty minutes' walk from the Underground Station a very traditional Tokyo, with old houses and little shops can be found on the island of Tsukudajima. Visitors who are not averse to this walk and who are willing to look around on their own, even at the risk of getting lost – and there are, after all, always taxis! – should take the opportunity of getting to know this little island in Tokyo Bay.

Location
Tokyo Bay

Underground Station
Tsukiji (Hibiya Line)

*Ueno Park   F2

Ueno Park is one of the most popular attractions in the city of Tokyo. It is criss-crossed by gravel paths. On the reed-fringed Shinobazu Pond boats can be hired for trips around a little island with its Bentendo Temple. Hot-dog sellers advertise their wares with loudspeakers, and there are many cinemas and amusement centres in the vicinity.

It is the largest park in Tokyo (212 acres; 85 ha). With its zoo and aquarium it is a real park for the people, but it is also a cultural centre with a number of museums, many temples, shrines and pagodas and some important public buildings.

Once part of a Daimyo's residence, the Park came into the possession of the Tokugawa in the early 17th c. In 1924 it was handed over to public ownership.

In 1868 Kannei-ji, which had been built by the Tokugawa as a domestic temple, was the last stronghold of the troops remaining loyal to the Shogun. In the course of the fighting everything was destroyed except for a five-storey pagoda. There is a memorial to the fallen who fought for the Emperor and a bronze statue of Saigo Takamori (1827–77), one of the leaders of the Meiji Restoration. As a general of Emperor Maiji's troops he conducted the war against Korea, but came into conflict with the central government. Consequently he became a leader of the Kagoshima Rebellion. When it was put down he committed "Seppuku" (ritual suicide) in accord with the Samurai code of honour. Nowadays he is, however, revered as a national hero. A flight of stone steps with many cherry trees on either side (see photograph on p. 91) leads up to the

District
Taito-ku

Underground Station
Ueno-ku (Ginza Line)

Railway Station
Ueno (Yamanote Line)

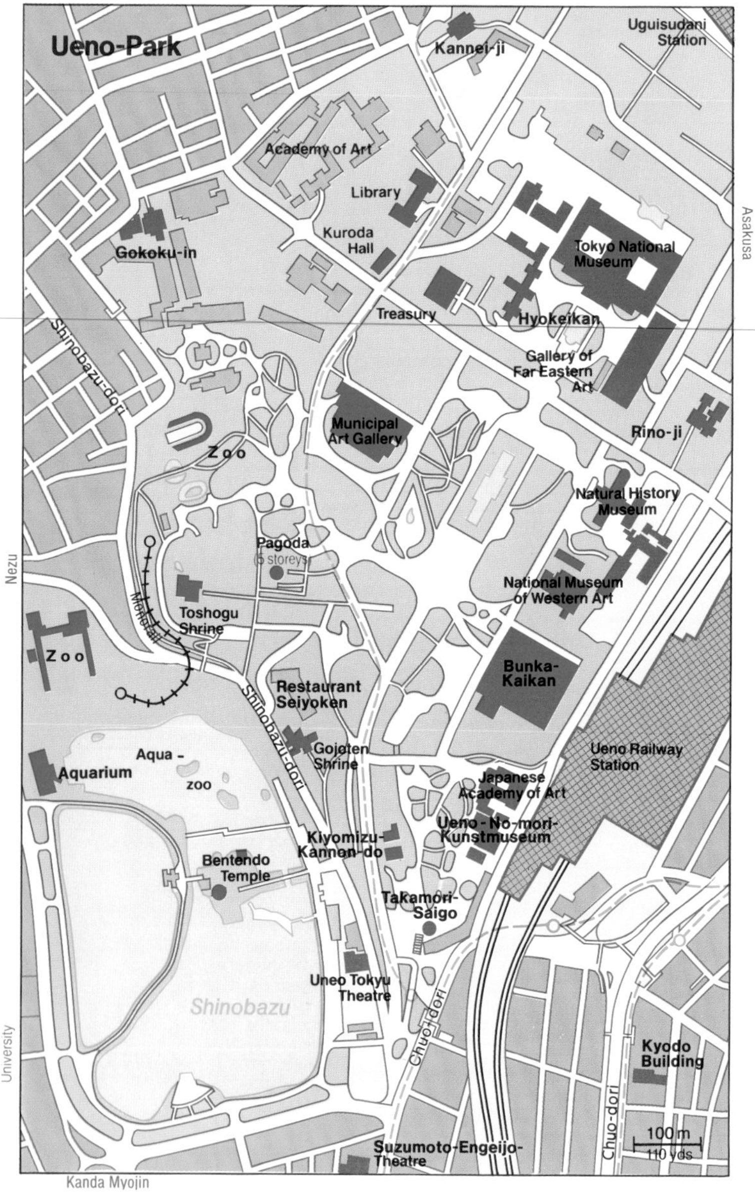

Ueno-Park

Uguisudani Station

Kannen-ji

Academy of Art

Library

Kuroda Hall

Gokoku-in

Treasury

Tokyo National Museum

Hyokeikan

Gallery of Far Eastern Art

Shinobazu-dori

Municipal Art Gallery

Rino-ji

Zoo

Natural History Museum

Nezu

Pagoda (5 storeys)

Monorail

Toshogu Shrine

National Museum of Western Art

Zoo

Shinobazu-dori

Restaurant Seiyoken

Bunka-Kaikan

Aqua-zoo

Aquarium

Gojoten Shrine

Japanese Academy of Art

Ueno Railway Station

Bentendo Temple

Kiyomizu-Kannon-do

Ueno-No-mori-Kunstmuseum

Takamori-Saigo

Shinobazu

Uneo Tokyu Theatre

University

Chuo-dori

Kyodo Building

Suzumoto-Engeijo-Theatre

Chuo-dori

100 m
110 yds

Kanda Myojin

Asakusa

Pagoda in Ueno Park

Takamori Saigo Monument in Ueno Park

memorial and the inscriptions. (The cherry trees are in blossom in early April.)
On the left-hand side lies the Kiyomizu Temple, modelled on the temple of the same name in Kyoto (see entry).

Near the Shinobazu Pond lie the extensive grounds of the zoo; another section of it is to be found between the Toshugo Shrine and the Tokyo Arts University, and the two parts are linked by a monorail. The zoo was opened in 1882, which makes it Japan's oldest zoo. It cannot perhaps be said to come up to the highest international standards, but it has two famous pandas. These are the gift of the People's Republic of China. When from time to time one of them dies, a replacement is sent over from China as a gesture of friendship. The death of a panda is always a matter for great sadness among school children, but then there is great rejoicing when the new mascot arrives.
The Aqua-Zoo on the N shore is one of the largest aquaria in the Far East.

Zoo

Of the public buildings in the Park the following are worthy of mention:
Tokyo Metropolitan Festival Hall. This modern building dates from 1961; it has a large and a small auditorium (holding 2327 and 611 spectators respectively). There are performances of operas here, as well as concerts (see Practical Information, Music).
The Ueno Library. This is a constituent part of the Library of Parliament and one of the largest libraries in Japan.

Public Buildings

Ueno Park

Temples and Shrines

As well as these buildings the Park also has a large number of small pagodas, temples and shrines. The Toshogu Shrine and the Kannei-ji Temple are the most notable among them.

Toshogu Shrine

The Toshogu Shrine is situated in the SW portion of the Park. A pathway with 256 bronze and stone lanterns on either side leads up to it. These were the gifts of various Daimyos. The Shrine was founded in 1627 in memory of Tokugawa Ieyasu. The present buildings date back to 1651.

The most important things to see here are the richly decorated Main Shrine and the five-storey pagoda of the Kannei-ji Temple. The latter was transferred here as the only building to survive the fighting which has been mentioned above. The Kara-mon Gate in front of the Main Shrine is said to have carvings by the famous sculptor Hidari Jingoro (17th c.).

Kannei-ji Temple

In the N part of the Park and E of the Tokyo Arts University may be found the new Kannei-ji. As the Choraku-ji Temple it used to stand in Serada, in the Prefecture of Gumma. After the destruction of the original Kannei-ji it was transferred here in 1875 as a replacement.

Museums

In Ueno Park's extensive grounds are to be found some of Tokyo's most famous museums – the Metropolitan Fine Art Gallery of Tokyo (see entry), the National Museum (see entry), the National Science Museum (see entry) and the National Museum of Western Art (see entry).

Yasukuni Shrine

Yasukuni Shrine   E4

The Yasukuni Shrine is in the Marunouchi District (see entry),
NW of Mizugami Park. It was built in the Shinto style in 1869
and is dedicated to Japan's war-dead. The entry to the outer
precinct is through two immense Torii. At the S entrance stands
a 39 ft (12 m) high granite Torii, and at the entry to the inner
precinct there is a bronze Torii 74 ft (22 m) high. Both of these
were put up in 1933.

The bronze statue on the left-hand side of the entry represents
Shinagawa Yajiro (1843–1900), a leading political figure of
the Meiji period.

The grounds of the Temple are beautiful with ginkgo trees and
ornamental cherries. This gave rise to the usual farewell of
soldiers departing for the war: "We'll meet again under the
cherries on Kudan Hill."

The spring festival at the shrine takes place between 21 and
23 April, the autumn festival from 17 to 19 October.

Yasukuni Shrine, in as much as it is a sanctuary for state
Shintoism, still gives rise to political contention. It was here that
with great secrecy the urns containing the remains of the men
condemned to death by the International Military Court in 1948
as war criminals were laid to rest. By this act of burial they
acquired the status of "hotoke", that is beings who were god-
like and deserving of reverence. For some time now the
ministers of the right-liberal government have been visiting the
Shrine.

Location
Kudan Kita, 3-chome
Shiyoda-ku, Marunouchi

Underground Station
Kudanshita (Tozai Line)

Chinatown in Yokohama

Yokohama – ocean-going ships in port

Yokohama

Location
18 miles (30 km) S

Railway
From Main Railway Station
(Tokaido; Yokosuka Line) to
Yokohama Station

or

From Main Railway Station
(Keihin–Tohoku Line) to
Sakura-Gicho Railway
Station of Kannai Railway
Station

Yokohama is a bustling, grey sea-port which, with Tokyo, is one of the centres of the Keihin Industrial Region (see Introduction, Commerce and Industry). This is a place which has no share in the chaste beauty of temples and gardens which is found everywhere else in Japan, yet it has a certain charm of its own. It was here that Japan opened its doors to the West in 1859 and allowed foreign settlements. When under Meiji rule Japan made the leap forward into modernity in the 19th c., the first railway to be built was the link between the cities of Tokyo and Yokohama. It was opened on 5 September 1872. The best way to get to Yokohama remains the railway. The Tokaido leaves Tokyo Main Station every half-hour, and the Yokosuka Express every fifteen minutes. The journey takes half an hour. The chief sights are Chinatown with its many little restaurants (where excellent meals may be eaten) and colourful shops, the famous Foreigners' Cemetery and the Sankei-en, a landscaped garden with an open-air museum.

Foreigners' Cemetery

Yokohama was and remains a place where Gaijin live. In the cemetery it is possible to decipher strange names and piece together strange destinies.

Sankei-en

This landscaped garden, on the S slopes of the foreigners' quarter, covers 50 acres (19 ha). It is well worth a visit during the flowering period, as it is renowned for its cherry and apricot blossom, its azaleas and water lilies.

Here, too, may be seen – in an open-air museum – reconstructed historical buildings, including a three-storey pagoda, reputedly more than 500 years old, which came from near Kyoto, a tea pavilion which the third Tokugawa Shogun Iemitsu had built, and a Daimyo villa from the feudal era.

Yushima seido (Confucian Shrine)   B5

The Yushima seido stands on rising ground not far from the Railway Station. It was founded in 1690, by the fifth Shogun Tsunayoshi. During the reign of the Tokugawa it developed into a centre of Confucianism. The Shrine has been repeatedly destroyed by fire, the last time during the catastrophic earthquake in 1923. The present buildings date from 1935. The bronzes of Confucius and other Chinese sages in the main hall are impressive.

Every year there is a festival in honour of Confucius on the last Sunday in April. Confucianism, which takes its name from the Chinese philosopher Confucius (551–479 B.C.) has, together with Shintoism and Buddhism, an important place (see Introduction, Population and Religion). In Confucianism humanity and the "five virtues of mutual love" are considered the highest principles.

District
Bunkyo-ku

Underground Station
Ochanomizu (Marunouchi Line)

Railway Station
Ochanomizu (Chuo-, Sobu Line)

*Zojoji Temple   E6

The five minutes' walk from the Underground Station to the Zojoji Temple leads through the delightfully laid-out Shiba Park which once formed part of the Temple complex. Founded in 1605 as the family temple of the Tokugawas, the temple belongs to the Jodo sect which assisted the Tokugawa clan in strengthening its Shogunate. Under the rule of that dynasty Japan shut itself off from the outside world for three centuries, developing in the meantime a despotic regime within the country.

The Temple and the Park around it were badly damaged by the 1923 earthquake and in the course of the Second World War. Only Sammon, the gate at the entrance, dates back to the period about 1605. The Hondo (Main Hall) of the temple which was founded in 1393 by the priest Shoso is a reconstruction dating only from 1974. This main hall is 115 ft (35 m) high and 158 ft (48 m) long.

Among the most impressive treasures of the temple are pictures from the time of the priest Honen, a black statue of the Buddha and the Great Temple Bell. In a precinct at the rear is one of the burial places of the Tokugawa Shoguns (the second is at Nikko, see entry).

Location
Shiba Park

Underground Station
Shiba–Koen (Hibiya Line)

Practical Information A to Z

Addresses

The following announcement from a hospital was inserted in the *Asahi Evening News*:

"Use the W exit from Ikebukuro Station. Keep to the main street for 540 yards (500 m), that is, for six minutes' walk. Then when you come to a filling station, turn right into a little side street with a tailor's shop on one side and a postbox on the other." It is more or less like this that Japanese tell their acquaintances the way to a temple or a shop. If possible they also provide a sketch-map. In Japan there are no addresses of the sort used in Europe.

Example

12–8–A Shiroganedai 5-chome Minato-ku is, for instance, a house or dwelling in the administrative district of Minato in Tokyo. This district is divided into sub-districts which have distinctive names which it is possible, with some effort, to make out on a good English-language plan of the city. Shiroganedai is one of them. Each sub-district is then further split up into blocks (chome). Then within the blocks the visitor must try to find the plot designated as 12–8, for there are, as may have been guessed, no house numbers either. On this plot stand several houses, and you have to look for the one that has the letter A. Accordingly you have to go round looking for a door with the nameplate of your acquaintance on it. It is a difficult business even for local postmen and taxi-drivers.

What visitors should do

Visitors are best advised to get every address written down for them on a card before they set out. The receptionists are quite used to requests for this particular service. Always write the telephone number as well as the address that you are looking for. Should the taxi-driver get lost, he can then call the number and ask for directions. Often signs are put up near to particular blocks which give the names of all the people living there, though these, of course, are in Japanese script.

Punctuality is expected. Allowances are made for foreign visitors who are bound to encounter more difficulties than the Japanese; even for them the city of Tokyo is a jungle.

Yet, since this is the case, it is vital to write all addresses correctly. If you do not do so you are sure to get lost – and neither will your letters arrive.

Airlines

Japan Air Lines

Tokyo Building (8 Floor)
7–3 Marunouchi, 2-chome, Chiyoda-ku.

Air Terminal

Tokyo City Air Terminal Co. Ltd,
Tokyo City Air Terminal Building,
Nihonbashi, Hakozaki-cho, Chuo-ku. Tel. 665–7111.
Here there is an enquiry desk where passengers can obtain

flight information, make bookings and reservations, hand in their luggage before departure (see entry) and buy their duty-free goods.

Deals with general enquiries and provides flight information. Tel. 665–7135.

Enquiry Desk

See entry

Airlines

See Arrival

Airports

Antiques

The Japanese are keen collectors, and have forced up prices in the country. There is hardly any chance of bargaining with an antique dealer. Care must be taken to avoid fakes.
Age and value do not always go together in Japan. Pieces which may be more modern but which are the work of a famed master or belong to a renowned school are often more expensive than older ones. Between 50,000 and 100,000 Yen is a reasonable price for a Samurai sword. Cast-iron vessels, wooden cabinets with metal fastenings, table-type ovens with a hollow for the charcoal or paintings on scrolls can often cost thousands, too. Genuine Netsuke (ebony figurines which were formerly used as ornamental buttons) are scarcely obtainable any more. The best things to look out for are woodcuts from the last two centuries.

The antique business has no centre in Tokyo. It is necessary to go to the big stores in which there are permanent art exhibitions. The following may also be recommended:

Specialist shops

Art Plaza Magatani
5–10-13, Toranomon, Minato-ku. Tel. 433–6321
Open: 10 a.m.–7 p.m.

Oriental Bazaar
9–13, Jingumae 5-chome, Shibuya-ku (Omotesando).
Tel. 400–3933

Nimi Sank odo
3–7-10, Toranomon, Minato-ku. Tel. 432-1358

Arrival

International air traffic is concentrated at the new Narita Airport. This came into operation in 1978; building took a long time, and there had been opposition on a large scale from the population affected. The airport lies some 37 miles (60 km) NE of Tokyo. Links with the centre of Japan's capital city are by various forms of public transport.

Narita Airport

Passengers travelling on an internal Japanese flight or flying on to other Japanese cities (e.g. Osaka, Nagoya, Okinawa Island) land at Haneda Airport. This is an older airport, situated some 9 miles (15 km) from the city centre, on Tokyo Bay. Apart from internal services it is only used for VIPs from abroad on official visits, and flights to and from China.

Haneda Airport

Practical Information

Suggestion

Before passing through customs travellers must complete customs forms in English. These may be found lying on tables or else may have been handed out in advance on the plane. If this is not the case, as often happens on Japan Airlines flights, passengers should ask the air hostess for a form. The name of the passenger's firm should be noted alongside his profession, and any unaccompanied baggage should in particular be declared. In most instances an oral declaration is sufficient for hand baggage. (There is some uncertainty over this: there are variations in the forms and declarations required.)

The rigorous safety measures at Narita are explained by the protest action taken over the years mainly by farmers from the vicinity who have opposed the Japanese state in a series of spectacular demonstrations. Security checks are always being made.

Hotel reservations

Tokyo is a metropolis in which it is necessary neither to look far for a hotel nor book in advance. Most of the hotels are, moreover, situated really centrally, mainly around the Ginza, or in the shopping and entertainment centres of Shinjuku, Shibuya, Akasaka or Ueno (see Hotels).

Narcotics, drugs

The possession of narcotics is a serious offence in Japan. Anybody caught with them receives a severe punishment. Customs officers make a thorough search for any contraband. Visitors should therefore be "clean" when they enter the country; otherwise they are running the risk of going to prison before they have even begun their stay in Japan.

Transfer to the city

There are several ways of getting into the city of Tokyo, which lies some 37 miles (60 km) away:

Skyliner: Passengers from the airport can take a bus which bears the sign "Skyliner" or else "Keisei".

Near the driver will be found a box into which the passenger tosses coins to the value of 130 Yen. From now on visitors will come across few Japanese who speak English. After about six minutes the bus arrives at the airport railway station of Keisei. Here passengers take an escalator down to a ticket office where a ticket with a seat number can be purchased. Coach and seat numbers are clearly marked.

The Skyliner departs every half-hour. Exactly one hour's journey takes passengers to Ueno, a district of Tokyo city. (Please note that the last train leaves Keisei Railway Station about 8.30 p.m.)

This is undoubtedly the quickest and cheapest way of getting to Tokyo.

From the station it is best to take a taxi to your hotel or whatever other destination you are looking for. If you show the driver the address there will be no problems. If you leave the train at Ueno, taxis will be found just to the left of the barrier where tickets must be handed in (so don't throw them away!)

Express Coach: These leave the airport every 5–10 minutes. They stop at the larger hotels and at Tokyo and Shinjuku Railway Stations, terminating at the Tokyo City Air Terminal (see entry) in the centre of the city. The fare is about 2000 Yen. The disadvantage is that the journey can take more than four hours when the expressway and the other roads are crowded. Generally, however, the journey takes between $1\frac{1}{2}$ and $1\frac{3}{4}$ hours.

Taxi: Travelling by taxi can likewise take a long time. The price is comparatively high, too, and can amount to as much as 20,000 Yen.

Babysitters

Babysitting is generally organised by the hotel. If that is not possible, there is an agency to help:
Tokyo Domestic Service
2–23, Akasaka, Minato-ku. Tel. 584-4769.

Normally the first three hours cost 3000 Yen. Each extra hour costs 1000 Yen.   Rates

Banks (Ginko)

Travellers cheques are not accepted in all banks. It is therefore best to go either to a foreign bank or else to one of the large branches of one of the major banks.
It is advisable to change money for a visit before leaving home as the rate of exchange is more favourable.

Mon.–Fri. 9 a.m.–3 p.m.; Sat. 9 a.m.–noon.   Opening times

Baths

The Japanese bath, according to reputation, is full of boiling hot water where both sexes bathe together unashamed. That is something that disappeared long ago. At first, to satisfy the requirements of the new legislation, a rope would be strung across the bath so that the bathhouse was at least not optically divided up. But now communal baths are to be found only in remote districts of Japan.
In Tokyo there are still several public bathhouses in the city which remain open until about midnight. Bathers undress before going into the bath and plunge into the water with only a little towel on. This the Japanese handle very deftly.
In no circumstances may bathers plunge straight into the pool. Instead they must soap themselves thoroughly and rinse themselves down well. Bathers clean up on a little wooden stool, and there is a bucket for rinsing.
Bathers who are not used to the heat should take care about plunging into the main basin over which hangs a cloud of steam. Those with heart complaints should avoid this altogether. In the bath there will be some Japanese, sitting there and sizing up the foreigner with great curiosity. It is not wise to spend more than 15–20 minutes in the hot bath. But then it will probably become evident that the muscles have been delightfully relaxed and that the coldness of a winter day has been driven out of the system. There is a reason why so many Japanese like to get into the hot baths of an evening; a bathhouse is the meeting-place of a neighbourhood. There people talk politics, swap the latest gossip, make friends and forget the day's toil.

See A–Z, Hot Springs   Hot springs

Beauticians

Beautician/Hair salons

A selection of beauty parlours which cater for foreign customers:

André Bernard
Horaiya Building (4th floor)
5–2–1 Roppongi, Minato-ku. Tel. 404–0616.

Max Beauty Salon
Takano Building (5th floor)
Tsunohazu, Shinjuku-ku. Tel. 354–5211.

Ohba Beauty Salon
Imperial Hotel. Tel. 503–8078.
Hotel Grand Palace. Tel. 263–6468.

Pink Pearl
Palace Hotel. Tel. 211–6975.

Shiseido Ginza Biyo-Shitsu
7–8 Ginza. Tel. 571–1821.

Takara Beauty Salon
7–1 Akasaka, Minato-ku. Tel. 402–2726.

Yonekura
Hotel Okura. Tel. 481–8011.

Appointments should always be booked in advance by telephone. There are other beauty parlours and hair salons in all the big stores and also in the big hotels.

Cosmetic surgery

Cosmetic surgery is advertised on TV, and those who have profited from it smile out at you from posters. Surgeons are always thinking of new shapes for noses. Cosmetic surgery is prescribed on a large scale in the land of the rising sun, and in Tokyo operations are extremely cheap and are carried out in every conceivable fashion.
The modern Japanese miss will have her quite delightful little Mongolian folds of skin smoothed away, so that she no longer has slit-eyes, has her nose stretched and her bosom rounded out. Some girls have this done as frequently as others buy themselves new clothes. So one of the favourite guessing games in Japan is trying to imagine how this or that star will appear on the screen after she has been on holiday for a week.

Box offices

Tickets for cultural events – concerts, etc. – are obtained from:

Playguide Service
Isetan Department Store (6th floor),
14–1, Shinjuku-ku. Tel. 352–1111. Ext. 3141.

Sukiyabashi Playguide
New Ginza Building (1st floor),
7–3–13, Ginza, Chuo-ku. Tel. 573–3675.

Akagiya Playguide
2–7-1, Nihonbashi, Chuo-ku. Tel. 273–5481.

Odakyu Department Store (1st floor)
1–3, Nishi-Shinjuku, Shinjuku-ku. Tel. 343–4807.

Seibu Department Store
1–1, Jingu-dori, Shibuya-ku. Tel. 462–0621.

Kyuko Playguide
5–7-4, Ginza, Chuo-ku. Tel. 571–0401.

Breakdown service

With hire cars the hire firm (see Car Hire.) should always be informed of a breakdown.

Calendar of events

1–3 January: New Year. When the weather is good, the sky over Tokyo is a silky blue. Businesses are shut, and so are all public buildings. Air pollution is noticeably reduced. The populace makes pilgrimages to the temples and shrines which are all decorated for the festive season. The Meiji Shrine and the Asakusa Kannon Temple are particularly crowded at this time. At the Yasukuni Shrine in Kuda, Chiyoda-ku, Noh theatre and Koto music and dance can be enjoyed.

January

2 January: New Year visit to the Imperial Palace. The Palace Garden is opened to the public from 9 a.m.–3 p.m. The Emperor appears several times on the palace balcony to greet the crowds.

6 January: Dezome Shiki. The Tokyo Fire Brigade New Year parade takes place in the Harumi district of the city. Acrobatic displays on ladders are a riveting spectacle.

15–16 January: Antiques fair of the streets of Seta-gaya-ku.

3 February: Setsubun, the "Bean Throwing Festival". On what, according to the old Japanese lunar calendar, used to be the last day of the year, there is bean throwing, to scare off the devil. This ancient folk festival is celebrated at all the temples and shrines. The Sensoji Temple in Asakusa, the Zojoji Temples in Shiba (near Tokyo Tower) and the Hie Shrine in Akasaka (near the Hilton Hotel) are especially worth visiting on this day.

February

25 February: start of the Plum Festival (Ume Matsuri), which continues until 15 March at the Yushima Tenjin Shrine in Bunkyo-ku (Underground: Yushima). The plum blossom is really beautiful. Every Saturday and Sunday the tea ceremony (Nodate) is performed in the open air.

3 March: Hina Matsuri (Dolls' festival). In earlier times only male children were respected. Dolls are displayed in fine costumes.

March

3 and 4 March: Daruma Ichi. The Daruma Market is held in the Jindaiji Temple in Chofu (Railway: Chofu). Thousands of Daruma figures are displayed, while Japanese music is played and Japanese dances performed.

2nd Sunday in March: Hi watari. The festival is celebrated in Kotsu Anzen Kito-cho on Mount Takao. Priests from the highland monastery walk bare-foot over the glowing embers of a fire which has been lit for the souls of the departed.

18 March: Kinryu-no-mai. Dragon dance in the Asakusa Kannon Temple (Underground: Asakusa) at 2 and 4 p.m. At the same time there is a parade.

26 March: Sakura Matsuri. Start of the cherry blossom festival in Ueno Park which continues until about 15 April.

April

8 April: Hana Matsuri. Flower festival in all temples on the occasion of the Buddha's birthday. A white elephant modelled in papier mâché is borne along in procession, and all the statues of the Buddha are decked with flowers. The Sensoji Temple in Asakusa is particularly worth a visit during this festival.

9 April: Shirasagi-no-mai. Dance of the white heron at the Asakusa Kannon Temple, at 11 a.m. and 1 p.m.

9–16 April: Kamakura Matsuri. Festival at the Hachiman Shrine in Kamakura with a parade in historic costumes, a Mikoshi parade with portable shrines and also a "Yabusame", an archery competition with the bowmen mounted on galloping horses (on the last day).

21–23 April: Spring Festival at the Yasukuni Shrine.

29 April: Birthday of the Emperor. The Emperor appears behind a window for a few minutes to the crowd which has been waiting since dawn.
Spring festival at the Meiji Shrine with performances of classical Japanese dances, Bugaku and Noh. The festival goes on until 3 May. On the last day there is a Japanese archery competition.

May

3 May: Yokohama minato Matsuri. A harbour festival in celebration of the opening of Yokohama harbour to foreign ships. At 11 a.m. an international parade sets out from Yamashita-koen (Park), arriving about 2 p.m. at Maita-koen (Park).

5 May: Children's (or more specifically Boys') Day. Happy parents hang up brightly coloured carp made of cloth which flutter in the breeze.

14 and 15 May: Kanda Festival at the Myojin Shrine in Kanda, the part of Tokyo city where the university is situated and the bookshops are to be found. Gigantic harps, which recall the feudal period, are carried along through the streets.

19 and 20 May: Sanja Matsuri, one of the greatest popular festivals in Tokyo. In the Asakusa temple precincts (near Asakusa Station on the Ginza Underground Line), portable

shrines are carried around amidst cries of delight (Mikoshi Procession) and lion dances are performed. There is a great parade of Geishas and Binzasaramai dancers.

20 and 21 May: Minato Matsuri. In Yokosuka on the Miura peninsula there is a great parade with wind bands and folk dancing. There is also a procession of portable shrines (Mikoshi).

9 and 10 June: Hozuki-ichi cherry market in the precinct of the Sensoji Temple in Asakusa. Branches of cherry blossoms decked with fruit and windmills are on sale.

June

10–16 June: Sanno Matsuri. Procession around the Hie Shrine in Akasaka Mitsuke (near the Hilton Hotel) with dramatic performances, dances and tea ceremonies in the open air (every other year only).

13–16 July: Mitama Matsuri. Festival of Remembrance for Souls of the Dead. According to Buddhist belief, the souls of the dead visit the earth at this time. In the cemeteries, and in homes, too, little lights burn in their honour. There are Bonodo-re performances and classical dancing, and about 6000 lanterns are hung up at the Yasukuni Shrine.

July

17 July: Edo-shumi Horyo Taikai. Start of the summer evening festival which continues until 15 August, on the shores of the Shinobazu Pond and also in the precinct around the pagoda in Ueno Park.

28 July: Hanabi Taikai. Evening firework display (7–9 p.m.) on the River Edo, near Shibsamata Square.

Early August: Fireworks in Keio Tamagawa on the River Tamagawa. These can also be viewed from boats.

August

13–15 August: Festival of the Shrines (Matsuri) in Fukagawa.

16 September: Yabusame. Festival at the Hachiman Shrine in Kamakura. There is a Japanese archery competition in which the bowmen wear historical costumes and have to shoot arrows while galloping by on horse-back.

September

1–10 October: Festival of the Foundation of the city of Tokyo, a celebration which first took place in 1956 when the city was 500 years old. Among the most spectacular events are the Tokyo Harbour Festival, the Miss Tokyo Competition, a parade of decorated floats, and lantern procession and various displays.

October

11–12 October: Oeshiki Festival at the Hommonji Temple. In commemoration of Nitchiren, a Buddhist monk, the faithful go to the temple on the night of 12 October, bearing great lanterns which are decorated with paper flowers.

17–19 October: Autumn Festival at the Yasukuni Shrine with performances of classical dances, Noh plays and an archery competition.

18 October: Kiryu-no-mai. A dragon dance at the Asakusa Kannon Temple.

31 October: Autumn Festival at the Meiji Shrine. This goes on until 3 November, a Japanese harvest festival. The programme includes performances of classical music and dances, Noh and Bugaku plays, Japanese archery, Aikido and Dakyu.

November

3 November: Daimyo Gyoretsu. Procession in historical costumes of the Edo Period in the Hakone-Yumoto district. Shirasagi-no-mai. Dance of the white heron at the Asakusa Kannon Temple in Asakusa (near the Ginza Underground Station). Festival in honour of the birthday of the Meiji-tenno at the Meiji Shrine.

15 November: Shichi-go-san. Day of the Children who are seven, five or three years old. Children and their parents dressed in their best clothes visit the Shrines.

Other events in November:
Tori-no-ichi: Hen Markets at the Otori Shrine in Asakusa. These take place on the Day of the Hen whenever it falls according to the Asiatic Zodiacal calendar. Particularly typical are the sale of "kumade" (bears' paws), bamboo rakes which are decorated in various ways.

December

14 December: Gishi Sai. Festival of the 47 Ronin at the Sengakuji Temple in Minato-ku.

17–19 December: Hagoita Ichi. Market at the Asakusa Kannon Temple in Asakusa. The sale of battledores for New Year is characteristic.

31 December: Omisoka. The great Old Year's Day Festival. The temple bells chime 108 times – 107 for the sins of the Old Year and one for the New Year. On this day the Zojoji Temple in Shiba and the Asakusa Kannon Temple are especially worth visiting.

Car hire

An International Driving Licence is needed. In Tokyo vehicles travel on the left but there is considerable overcrowding on many main roads. Road signs in English are few and far between. Even Japanese often get lost. The highest average speed you can count on amounts to no more than 9 miles (15 km) an hour (see Motoring).

Car hire firms

Visitors who are prepared to venture forth can hire cars from the following:
Nissan Rent-a-car. Tel. 586–2301.
Toyota Rent-a-car. Tel. 463–6923.
Hertz have a number of branches in Tokyo.

Information

It is advisable to ask for information at the reception desk of your hotel.

Chemists (Yakyoku, Kusuriya)

American Pharmacy
Hibiya Park Building,
1–8-1, Yurakucho, Chiyoda-ku. Tel. 271–4036.
Open: Mon.–Sat. 9 a.m.–7 p.m.; Holidays: 11 a.m.–6 p.m.
Closed: Sun.

English understood

Hibiya Pharmacy
Mitsui Building,
1–1-2, Yurakucho, Chiyoda-ku. Tel. 501–6377.
Open: Mon.–Fri. 9.10 a.m.–7.20 p.m.; Sat. 9.10 a.m.–5.30 p.m.
Closed: Sun.; Holidays.

Fuji Pharmacy
Sankei Building,
1–7-2, Otemachi, Chiyoda-ku.
Open: Mon.–Fri. 8.30 a.m.–6.30 p.m.; Sat. 9 a.m.–5 p.m.
Closed: Sun.; Holidays.

Medicines without
prescriptions

Many medicines are available in Japan without prescription. If
you know what medicine it is that you need, there may well be
no need to consult a doctor.

The great majority of medicines have directions for use in
English.

Directions for use

Generally between 10 a.m. and 6 p.m.

Opening times

Church Services

Only 1% of the Japanese population is Christian. So Christian
churches are not numerous. For the most part services are
conducted in English. Here are two addresses.

Franciscan Chapel Centre
2–37, Roppongi, 4-chome, Minato-ku. Tel. 401–2141.

Catholic

St Paul's International Lutheran Church
1–2-32, Fujimicho, Chiyoda-ku. Tel. 261–3740.

Protestant

Cinemas

Japan is an important country for film production, and the
Japanese are keen cinema-goers. Most foreign films only have
Japanese subtitles and are shown with their original sound
tracks; this is a big advantage for foreign visitors. The last
programmes begin about 7 p.m.; generally people go to the
cinema during the day time. Prices are relatively high.
Even visitors who cannot understand Japanese can gain
insight into Japanese daily life by going to see Japanese films.
So it is a good idea to go to
Film Service Center,
11, Kyobashi 3-chome, Chuo-ku. Tel. 561–0823.
Many classical Japanese films are shown here, and the prices

are modest. Information about what is showing – and about the programmes of the cinemas in central Tokyo – may be found in the English-language newspapers.

Climate

Tokyo lies in the same latitude as Crete and Teheran. There are four distinct climatic seasons:

Winter comprises the months from December to February. As well as (very rare) snow and frost there are often cloudless skies and sunshine.

Spring is from March to May. This is a favourable season for a stay in Tokyo, as the weather can be mild and warm.

In the summer, that is the months from June to August, visitors should on no account go to Tokyo. Temperatures are high, the humidity is oppressive, and monsoon rains and storms are frequent.

Autumn is from September to November. This is the most suitable time for a visit to Tokyo. It is warm, mild and pleasant. Unfortunately, however, this is also the season for a series of typhoons which blow up from the south. They are all given numbers. Sometimes they are dangerous.

Clothing

Waterproofs are worn invariably in every season of the year, except in winter. As Tokyo is situated on the same latitude as Las Vegas, Teheran or Crete, it has a relatively warm climate. But its precipitation rate is more than twice the average for most parts of Europe. The worst weather is encountered during the typhoon season, that is to say more or less during the months of August and September. There are not only dangerous storms but also unpleasantly high humidity. As the temperatures are also high at that time, the summer is, therefore, the worst season for a visit. Warm clothing is needed only during the brief, and not excessively chilly, winter. This season is recommended for a visit since the skies are clear.

Footwear

Shoes are removed when making visits and also when going into temples. It is, therefore, a good idea to take slip-on shoes to Japan; otherwise when you are out with a party you hold up everything while your are tying up your laces. Visitors who take shoes that are size 9 (43) or larger should not count on being able to purchase new shoes in Japan.

Garment sizes

Ladies' Outer Garments

Japan	9	11	13	15	17	19	21
England	32	34	36	38	40	42	44
Europe (Continent)	38	40	42	44	46	48	50

Gentlemen's Outerwear (Suits, Coats, Pullovers, etc.)

		S		M		L	LL
Japan							
England	34	36	38	40	42	44	46
Europe	44	46	48	50	53	54	56

Shirts (Collar Size)

Japan	36	37	38	39	40	41	42
England	14	$14\frac{1}{2}$	15	$15\frac{1}{2}$	16	$16\frac{1}{2}$	17
Europe (Continent)	36	37	38	39	40	41	42

Changing room at entrance to a shrine

Ladies' Shoes

Japan	23	23¾	24	24½	25	25½	25¾
England	4½	5	5½	6	6½	7	7½
Europe	36	37	38	38	38	39	40

Gentlemen's Shoes

Japan	24½	25¾	26	26¾	27½	28	29
England	5	6	7	8	9	10	11
Europe	39	40	41	42	43	44	45

Currency regulations

There are no restrictions of any sort on entry. Japanese Yen up to a value of 5 million may be taken out of the country.

Import and export

Coins are issued as follows:
1 Yen in aluminium
5 Yen in brass, with a hole
10 Yen in bronze
50 Yen in cupro-nickel with a hole
100 Yen in cupro-nickel
500 Yen in cupro-nickel
Notes are issued in the following denominations:
500, 1000, 5000, 10,000 and 100,000 Yen.

Currency

£1 is worth approximately 260 Yen (March 1986)
$1 is worth approximately 179 Yen (March 1986)

Rate of exchange

see Banks

Exchanges

107

Practical Information

A display of Japanese-style dishes

Poisson mort – sea-food delicacies

Cuisine

Visitors will recognise very quickly that Japanese cuisine is a feast for the eye. Everything is characterised by its colour and is very cleanly prepared.
Out of the many dishes available, the following are especially remarkable:

Japanese specialities

Gossamer-thin slices of meat are dipped with chopsticks into boiling soup containing vegetables. The meat and the vegetables are then covered in sauce.

Shabu-shabu

Corn noodles with various additional ingredients, garnished with all manner of different trimmings. Similar to spaghetti.

Soba

Thin slices of meat cooked in an iron pot with mushrooms, young turnips and other vegetables.

Sukiyaki

Various sorts of raw fish or else squid, shrimps and so on are dipped into soya sauce on balls of soured rice before being eaten. The easiest way to eat this dish is with your fingers.

Sushi

It was the Portuguese who brought this habit of cutting fish, meat or vegetables into thin slices, covering it in batter and frying it.

Tempura

Squid, tuna and other sorts of fish are cut into thin slices and are eaten raw, having first been dipped into a sauce which the diner has himself prepared.

Sashimi

Another Japanese noodle dish. The noodles are generally served in a large dish with broth which sometimes also contains meat, fish or vegetables.

Udon

A deep-fried pork cutlet is eaten with raw, grated cabbage.

Tonkatsu

Small pieces of chicken, liver and vegetables are speared on a skewer and then grilled over a charcoal fire. It is excellent as a snack.

Yakitori

There is a touch of the West in all these dishes, and in Tokyo there are masses of Western restaurants which are run by Japanese. Western food in every form has been adopted by the Japanese for years; as early as the 19th c. Japan began to follow American and European fashions.
Visitors who want to see what real Japanese food is like must take a guide; otherwise they will not get far either with ordering or with the various practices dictated by etiquette.

Suggestion

See entry

Food and drink

See entry

Restaurants

Cultural Events

Ikebana and the Tea Ceremony (see entries, A–Z), features of the Japanese lifestyle which never fail to amaze and delight visitors from Europe, are taught in a great number of schools. Foreigners are welcome to visit these and learn about these arts. Advance notice is required. Visitors can either have arrangements made by their hotel or else they can make contact direct with one of the following institutions:

Ikebana

Ikenobo Ochanomizu School. Tel. 292–3071.
Railway and Underground: Ochanomizu.
Lessons: Mon., Wed., Fri. 2–4 p.m.

Sogetsu School. Tel. 408–1126.
Underground: Aoyama-Ichome.
Lessons: Tues. 10 a.m.–noon; 1.30–3 p.m

Ohara School. Tel. 499–1200.
Underground: Omotesando.
Lessons: Mon.–Fri. 10 a.m.–noon.

Tea Ceremony

Imperial Hotel's Tokoan. Tel. 504–1111, Extension 5858.
Underground: Hibiya.
Displays: daily (except Sun. and holidays) 10 a.m.–noon; 1–4 p.m.

Hotel Okura's Choshoan. Tel. 582–0111.
Underground: Toranomon.
Displays: daily 11 a.m.–noon; 1–4.30 p.m.

Hotel New Otani's Seiseian. Tel. 265–1111.
Underground: Akasaka-Mitsuke.
Railway: Yotsuya.
Displays: Thurs., Fri, Sat. 11 a.m.–noon; 1–4 p.m.

Tea Room of Suntory Museum of Art. Tel. 470–1073.
Underground: Akasaka Mitsuke.
Displays: Tues.–Sun. 1.30–4 p.m.

Tea Room of the Yamatane Museum of Art. Tel. 669–3211.
Underground Kayabacho.
Displays: Tues.–Sun. 11 a.m.–5 p.m.

Customs regulations

Entry

The allowance is 400 cigarettes or 2 lb (500 g) of tobacco or 100 cigars, as well as three bottles of spirits and presents up to a total value of not more than 100,000 Yen.
The following must not be brought into Japan: narcotics, pornographic magazines and books.
Permission must be sought to import the following: certain sorts of plants, weapons, explosives and swords.
Special official approval is needed for the importation into Japan of such animals as dogs, cats and other household pets.

Dentists

Dentist (Shi-ka, Ha-isha)

English understood:
Royal Dental Clinic
Dr T. Ono,
Komuro Bldg, 2nd floor,
4-10-11, Roppongi, Minato-ku. Tel. 404–0819.

Hardy Barracks Dental Clinic
8-11-37, Akasaka, Minato-ku. Tel. 408-2002.

Empire Dental Clinic
Dr Kubo,
28, Kaikyo-cho, Shinjuku-ku. Tel. 356-2910, 356-2926.

Amano Dental Clinic
Kyowa Bldg., 1st floor,
1-18-13, Shibashi, Minato-ku. Tel. 501-0883.

Aoyama Mansion Dental Clinic
Aoyama Mansion, 2nd floor,
3-8-38, Minami-Aoyama, Minato-ku. Tel. 408-3501.

Aoyama Dental Clinic
Asahi Seimei Bldg, 3rd floor,
1-7-8, Shibuya, Shibuya-ku. Tel. 407-7155.

Ohba Dental Clinic
Olympia Annex 203,
6-31-21, Jingumae, Shibuya-ku. Tel. 409-7155.

Takeoshi Dental Clinic
24-8, Sakuragaoka, Shibuya-ku. Tel. 461-3655.

Departure

It is absolutely essential to allow three hours for the journey out
to Narita airport and for all the departure formalities.
It is best to hand in all luggage at the Air Terminal (see Air
Terminal).
Address: Hakozaki-cho. Tel. 665-7111.
In the Terminal there is a Duty Free Shop where passengers
should complete their purchases. It often happens that,
because of late arrival of the coach at the airport, there is hardly
another opportunity.
When making last-minute purchases and, if need be, changing
Japanese currency, remember that airport taxes have to be paid
on departure. Information about the amount applicable at the
time of the journey will be provided by the airline.
It is most convenient to travel out to the airport by the coach
that departs from the Air Terminal.
At the airport security precautions are strict and thorough.

Diplomatic and Consular Offices

1, Ichiban-cho, Chiyoda-ku, J-102 Tokyo. Tel. (03) 265 5511. United Kingdom Embassy

Holme Ringer and Co. Ltd, 9-9, Minato-machi, Moji-ku, J-801 Consulates
Kitakyushu. Tel. (093) 331 1311.

Hong Kong and Shanghai Bank Building, 45, Awaji-machi
4-chome, Higashi-ku, J-541 Osaka. Tel. (06) 231 3355.

10-5, Akasaka 1-chome, Minato-ku, J-107 Tokyo. Tel. United States of America
(03) 583 7141. Embassy

111

Practical Information

Consulates	5–26, Ohori 2-chome, Chuo-ku, J-810 Fukuoka. Tel. (092) 751 9331.
	10, Kano-cho 6-chome, Ikuta-ku, J-650 Kobe. Tel. (078) 331 6865.
	2129, Gusukuma, Urasoe City, J-901-21 Naha, Okinawa. Tel. (0988) 77 8142.
	Sankei Building (9th floor), 4–9, Umeda 2-chome, Kita-ku, J-530 Osaka. Tel. (06) 341 2754.
	Kita 1-jo, Nishi 28-chome, Chuo-ku, J-064 Sapporo. Tel. (011) 641 1115.
Canada Embassy	3–38, Akasaka 7-chome, Minato-ku, J-107 Tokyo. Tel. (03) 408 2101.

Doctors

Physician (Nai-Ka)	English understood:
	Taisei Clinic (Taisei Kenko Kanri Center) Shinjuku Center Building, 7th Floor North, 1–25, Nishi-Shinjuku, Shinjuku-ku. Tel. 348-1111. Consultations: Dr Sh. Nagano: Tues. 9 a.m.–noon.
Paediatrician (Shoni-Ka)	Dr H. Ono 2-10-41, Fujimi, Chiyoda-ku. Tel. 263-1371. Telephone for appointment (in the morning before 8 a.m. at the Police Hospital – Kesatsu-Byoin).
	Amano Shonika Tin Dr A. Amano Daiichi Aoyama Building, Kita-Aoyama, Minako-ku. Tel. 404-8770. Telephone for appointment.
Hospital	See entry

Earthquakes

The great Kanto earthquake of 1923 is still not forgotten, especially since there is supposed to be an earthquake of this severity every 60 years. Meantime Japan has installed a range of sophisticated early warning systems including seismographs anchored to the seabed. If there were to be an earthquake warning, it is, however, unlikely foreigners could understand it without assistance.

There are, however, many earthquakes in Japan, and visitors need not be too worried about them. All the same, it is best to be on one's guard. The cellars of the largest buildings offer some guarantee of safety, and supplies of water and food are laid on.

Emergency Calls

110	110 is the Emergency Call Number for the Police. Generally only Japanese is spoken. Sometimes somebody who speaks English can be called to the phone, but even then communication can be difficult.

119 is the Emergency Call Number for the Fire Brigade or the Ambulance Service. Even here there can be language problems in serious cases.

0051 is the number of the Telephone Exchange for International Calls. It is, it is true, not intended for emergency calls. But help would no doubt be provided if the matter is really urgent.

Excursions

The most interesting places to visit in Tokyo are listed alphabetically under Tokyo from A to Z and descriptions are given there.
For excursions which amount to city tours, see entry for Sightseeing.

Food and drink

It is well known that the Japanese eat with chopsticks ("o-hashi"). Visitors will be relieved to learn that in most of the restaurants ultra-refined eating habits are not expected. Soup may be served not at the start of the meal but during it or even at the end; in formal meals two soups are served. If foreigners cannot manage too well with chopsticks, nobody takes offence. It is always possible to ask for European cutlery. For this it is useful to note the following words:

Eating habits

foku=fork
naifu=knife
spun=spoon

All these words are, of course, based on English.
Tourists ought, however, to practise eating with chopsticks while still at home. Japanese chopsticks are almost invariably made of wood, and in cheap establishments the pairs are still joined at one end, which shows they have not been used before. The diner breaks the pair apart, stirs his sauce or cooks fish soup at table with them. In good restaurants proper lacquer-ware chopsticks are provided.
Visitors should, moreover, not opt every time for Japanese cooking as they wander across the city. The Italian restaurants in particular are very popular, and their prices are very acceptable in such an expensive city as Tokyo.

The water in Tokyo is clean and palatable, even when it comes from the mains, though it tastes strongly of chlorine. Visitors who are rather doubtful about drinking water when making an excursion in the country can ask for tea. If, however, it is a question of social drinking of alcoholic beverages, there are other reasons for being careful. Those who indulge in sake (rice wine) often end up with a hangover. The main reason for this is because the visitor is always offered larger and larger amounts of it. He is scarcely allowed to empty his glass before it is filled up again. In restaurants the people at the next table are often keen to fill your glass, and that is an excellent way of establishing new social contacts.

Drinking habits

The Japanese are great lovers of whisky because it has a foreign, that is to say an American, cachet. It is, however, usually drunk with a great deal of water.

There is a local spirit, distilled from what is left over when sake is made. It is called Shochu and its taste can hardly be described as pleasant. Western palates and thirsts find Awamori, made from sweet potatoes, more acceptable. Connoisseurs will not always care for Japanese wines, not just because they are expensive, but also because of an unusual taste. There are, however, a few excellent Japanese wines being produced.

Japan's beers are almost all good, especially such brands as Kirin, Sapporo and Suntory.

Visitors who don't stick to just water and milk need to know the word "kampai" – it means "cheers".

Foreigners in Japan

For many years Japan adopted a xenophobic attitude. Fishermen who had stayed too long at sea because of storms quickly fell under the suspicion of having established contact with seamen from other lands and had to expect to be punished. It is for this reason that even nowadays the children of fisherfolk find it difficult to marry into families that live inland. Travellers will no longer find much trace of such feelings of animosity towards foreigners. The Japanese have learned to live with the "foreign devils" who are always treated with every show of courtesy. But beneath their good manners there remains quite a lot of suspicion, and many Japanese still keep their distance. A foreigner who is invited to visit a Japanese in his own home has achieved something quite remarkable.

Galleries

Visitors who find themselves confused in a new world of artistic experiences will generally be gratified when they go in search of Japanese art in most of the galleries here. In the first place, the selection here is better than in many so-called museums, which suffer because state support is parsimonious, and, in the second, English-speaking advice may readily be obtained.

Idemitsu Gallery
1–1, 3-chome, Marunouchi, Chiyoda-ku.

Namiki-dori (it is next door to Ketel, the German restaurant).

Natenshi Gallery
11–3, Kyobashi, Chuo-ku.
Supplier to American and European museums and galleries. On the 3rd floor, sculptures and oil paintings. Specialises in contemporary art.

Yoseido Gallery
5–15 Ginza, 5-chome.
Yoseido is the only gallery in Tokyo to deal in modern Japanese lithographs, engravings and prints. About 130 artists are under commission to the gallery, and this fact is reflected in the prices.

"Gangsters" (Yakuzo)

The Japanese Police last conducted a census of "gangsters" in 1980. There were then 106,754 of them, in 2517 organised gangs. They are not really gangsters in the Western sense, but rather members of a kind of sub-culture, with their own code of honour, operating on the fringes of criminal areas and are encountered in all of Tokyo's gaming and drinking districts. Their appearance conforms to the classical American model, with white shoes and striped suits. They can also be recognised by their tattoos and sometimes by the fact that their little finger is missing. The latter will have been amputated either as a mark of their loyalty towards their boss or as the penalty for some abuse. In Japan gangsters may manage "love-hotels", small restaurants, patchinko parlours, etc. More rarely they are also active in illegal arms trading and drug peddling, but narcotics are uncommon in Japan. The largest gangster organisation is called Yamagumi-guchi. Its leaders are well known and even give interviews on TV. The police intervene mainly when gang warfare breaks out.

Consorting with gangsters does not bring disgrace. In 1978 Prime Minister Ohira, who is now dead, allowed his photograph to be published in the *Mainichi*, a daily paper, showing him arm in arm and drinking whisky with a well-known gangster boss.

Guides

Information about guides who can speak English may be obtained from
Japan Guide Association
Shinkokusai Building,
3–4–1, Marunouchi, Chiyoda-ku. Tel. 213–2706
Hotels and travel agents also put visitors in touch with English-speaking guides.

Information

For one day: 15,000 Yen.
For half-day: 12,000 Yen (1981 rates).

Rates

Hospitals (Byoin or Hospital)

Generally the hotel will be able to advise.

Hospitals in which some doctors and nurses speak English, in which all branches of medicine are represented and where outpatients are also treated are:

International Catholic Hospital (Seibo Byoin)
2–5–1, Nakaochiai, Shinjuku-ku. Tel 951–1111.

St Luke's International Hospital (Sei Luka Byoin)
10–1, Akashi-cho, Chuo-ku. Tel. 541–5151.

Tokyo Sanitarium Hospital (Eisei Byoin)
3–17-3, Amanuma, Suginami-ku. Tel. 392–6151.

Practical Information

Expressions

A few phrases may help you make yourself understood:

Byo-ki desu	I am ill
Hayaku kite kudasei	Please come quickly
Watakushiwa Igirisujin desu	I am British
Eigo shika wakarimasen	I can speak only English

Booklets

The newspaper company, Japan Times Ltd, has published a booklet containing a collection of phrases which are helpful and necessary when visiting a doctor. Visitors planning to stay for some time in Japan should obtain a copy of it either through the Foreign Travel Agency (see Information Offices) or else from the newspaper office itself (see Newspapers). The title of the booklet is "How to consult the doctor in five languages" (Japanese, English, French, German and Spanish).

Doctors

see entry

Hotels

General

Tokyo's hotels are excellent but expensive. As there is enough hotel accommodation available, advance booking is not indispensable. All the same, arrival (see entry) in Tokyo is much simpler if the visitor knows where he or she will be staying. The bigger hotels are all in the city centre. They have air-conditioning, and there are telephones in every room. Many hotels have their own arcade of shops.

Hotel Imperial

Luxury Hotels: a double room costs between 17,000 and 30,000 Yen.
Family Hotel: a double room costs between 9000 and 17,000 Yen.

*Imperial Hotel (1125 r.), 1-1-1, Uchisaiwaicho, Chiyoda-ku. Tel. 504–1111.
*Keio Plaza Inter Continental Hotel (1428 r.), 2-2-1, Nishi-Shinjuku, Shinjuku-ku. Tel. 344–01–11.
*The New Otani (2047 r.), 4–1, Kioicho, Chiyoda-ku. Tel. 265–1111.
*Hotel Okura (899 r.), 2-10-4, Toranomon, 2-chome, Minato-ku. Tel. 582–0111.
*Palace Hotel (404 r.), 1–1-1, Marunouchi, Chiyoda-ku. Tel. 211–5211.
*Tokyo Prince Hotel (484 r.), 3-3-1, Shiba Park, Minato-ku. Tel. 432–1111.
Akasaka Prince Hotel (738 r.). 1–2, Kioicho, Chiyoda-ku. Tel. 234–1111.
Akasaka Tokyu Hotel (566 r.), 2-14-3, Nagatacho, Chiyoda-ku. Tel. 580–2311.
Century Hyatt Tokyo (760 r.), 2-7-2, Nishi-Shinjuku, Shinjuku-ku. Tel. 349–0111.
Fairmont Hotel Tokyo (240 r.), 2-1-17, Kudan-Minami, Chiyoda-ku. Tel. 262–1151.
Hotel Kokusai Kanko (95 r.), 1-8-3, Marunouchi-Chiyoda-ku. Tel. 215–32811.
Hotel Pacific (954 r.), 3-13-3, Takanawa, Minato-ku. Tel. 445–6711.
Miyako Hotel Tokyo (483 r.), 1–1-50, Shiro-ganedai, Minato-ku. Tel. 447–3111.
Takanawa Prince Hotel (400 r.), 3-13-1, Takanawa, Minato-ku. Tel. 447–1111.
Tokyo Hilton International (838 r.), 6-6-2, Nishi-Shinjuku, Shinjuku-ku, Tel. 344–5111.

Hotel Daiei (82 r.) 1–15, Koishika-wa, Bunkyo-ku. Tel. 813–6271.
Diamond Hotel (162 r.), 25, Ichiban-cho, Chiyoda-ku. Tel. 263–2211.
Ginza Dai-Ichi Hotel (803 r.), 8–13-1, Ginza, Chuo-ku. Tel. 542–5311.
Ginza Nikko Hotel (112 r.), 8-4-21, Ginza, Chuo-ku. Tel. 571–4911.
Ginza Tokyu Hotel (445 r.), 5–15-9, Ginza, Chuo-ku. Tel. 541–2411.
Hotel Grand Palace (500 r.), 1–1-1, Iidabashi, Chiyoda-ku. Tel. 264–1111.
Haneda Tokyu Hotel (297 r.), 2–8-6, Haneda-kuko, Ota-ku. Tel. 747–0311.
Hill-Top-Hotel (89 r.), 1–1, Kanda Surugadai, Chiyoda-ku. Tel. 293–2311.
Marunouchi Hotel (208 r.), 1–6-3, Marunouchi, Chiyoda-ku. Tel. 215–2151.
Hotel New Japan (506 r.), 2-13-8, Nagata-cho, Chiyoda-ku. Tel. 581–5511.
Hotel New Meguro (31 r.), 1-3-18, Chuo-cho, Meguro-ku. Tel. 719–8121.
Shiba Park Hotel (300 r.), 1-5-10, Shiba, Minato-ku. Tel. 433–4131.

Shimbashi Dai-Ichi-Hotel (1300 r.), 1–2-6, Shimbashi, Minato-ku. Tel. 501–4411.

Hotel Takanawa (217 r.), 2–1-17, Takanawa, Minato-ku. Tel. 443–9251.

Takanawa Tobu Hotel (201 r.), 4–7-6, Takanawa, Minato-ku, Tel. 447–0111.

Takara Hotel (142 r.), 2–16-5, Higashi-Ueno, Taito-ku. Tel. 831–0101.

Hotel Tokyo (24 r.), 2–17-8, Takanawa, Minato-ku. Tel. 447–5771.

Tokyo Hotel Urashima (1001 r.), 2–5-23, Harumi, Chuo-ku. Tel. 533–3111.

Tokyo Kanko Hotel (158 r.), 4–8-10, Takanawa, Minato-ku. Tel. 443–1211.

Tokyo Station Hotel (62 r.), 9–1, 1-chome, Marunouchi, Chiyoda-ku. Tel. 231–2511.

Hotel Tokyukanko (48 r.), 2–21-6, Akasaka, Minato-ku. Tel. 582–0451.

Hotel Toshi Center (55 r.), 2–4-1, Hirakawa-cho, Chiyoda-ku. Tel. 265–8211.

Youth Hostels	See entry
Inexpensive accommodation	See entry
Ryokan	See entry

Ikebana

See A–Z, Ikebana, and also see Cultural Events

Inexpensive accommodation

The following offer simple and inexpensive accommodation:

English House
2–23-8, Nishi-Ikebukuro,
Toshima-ku. Tel. 982–4451.
The proprietor speaks English. Showers and cooking facilities for communal use. English House is about six minutes' walk from Mejiro Railway Station.

Okubo House
1–11-32, Hyakunincho,
Shinjuku-ku. Tel. 361–2348.
Visitors can choose between either a dormitory (as in a youth hostel) or a small single room with Japanese tatami mats. Okubo House closes at 11 p.m.

Yoshida House
1–25-25, Kasuga-cho,
Nerima-ku. Tel. 926–4563.
The rooms (tatami-matted) are all for two persons. Communal cooking and wash-room facilities.

Kimi Hotel
1034, 2–chome, Ikebukuro,
Toshima-ku. Tel. 971–3766.
Rooms with beds.

Ryokan Yashima
1–15-5, Hyakunincho,
Shinjuku-ku. Tel. 364–2534.

See entry	Youth Hostels
See entry	Hotels
See entry	Ryokan

Institutions

Japan Foundation
Park Building,
3, Kioi-cho, Chiyoda-ku. Tel. 263–4504.
Lectures and discussions, seminars, Japanese film weeks,
library with books in English.

Japanese institutions

Interpreters

Japan Convention Service
3–23, Roppongi 7-chome, Minota-ku. Tel. 401–1111.

Agencies

Japan Guide Association
Shin-Kokusai-Building,
4–1 Marunouchi 3-chome, Chiyota-ku. Tel. 213–2706.

Japan Lingua Service
2–9-13, Ginza, Chou-ku. Tel. 567–3814.

Language

Although the study of English forms part of the school
curriculum in Japanese schools, visitors will meet few
Japanese who can speak eigo-no (English) fluently. The
Japanese have little opportunity to practise the language, and
they generally understand better if you write down your
questions. If you do this, they will often prefer to reply in
writing. Because the Japanese language is a polysyllabic
language they often put a u or an o on the end of English words.
Thus the sentence "the cat has four legs" would be
pronounced "The catsu hasu folu legsu", the r often being
changed into an l.

It is therefore best to learn at least a few Japanese phrases.

Phrases

I am British	Watashi-wa Igirisujin desu
I am American	Watashi-wa Amerikajin desu
I am Canadian	Watashi-wa Kanadajin desu
Please telephone the	Taishikan ni denwa shite
Embassy	kudasei

Practical Information

How much is that? (Also – My bill, please)	Ikura-desuka?
I don't understand	Wakarimasen
Is there a police box nearby?	chikaku ni koban arimasu ka?
I am ill	byoki desu
How much does that cost?	kore ikura desuka?
Where is . . . ?	. . . wa doko desuka?
Where is the toilet?	toire wa doko desuka?
Goodbye	Sayonara
Car	kuruma
Railway Station	eki
Bank	ginko
Beer	biru
Please	dozo
Bus	basu
Thank you	arigato
I am sorry	sumimasen
Money	okane
Fish	sakana
Meat	niku
Good evening	konbanwa
Good day	konnichi-wa
Yes	hai
Coffee	kohi
Noon	hiru
Morning	asa
Afternoon	gogo
Night	yoru
Express way	lie
Taxi	takushii
Telephone	denwa
Tea (Japanese)	o-cha
Tea (Indian)	ko-cha
Ticket	kippu
Underground	chikatehtsu
Magazine	zasshi
Newspaper	shinbun

Lost property offices

Police	Lost Property Office in the City Police Headquarters 3–11-14, Minami Aoyama, Minato-ku. Tel 478–1547. It is advisable to go there accompanied by an interpreter. A visit to this Central Lost Property Office should be made only at the end of about a week, when all other possibilities have been exhausted.
Railway	Japan National Railways Main Railway Station (Tokyo eki). Tel. 231–1880.
Underground	Lost Property Office at Ueno Underground Station. Tel. 834–5577.
Private railways and buses	All property which is found is first taken to the terminus of the line in question. Central Lost Property Office. Tel. 216–2953.

Tokyo Taxi Kindaika Centre
Shinseikan Building,
Shinanoma-chi, Shinjuku-ku. Tel 355–0300.

Taxi Central Office

Massage

Visitors who seek complete relaxation through massage will be
delighted.
Every hotel will make arrangements for massage which is given
by qualified masseuses. For massage a thin cotton "evening"
kimono (Yukata) is worn. These garments are provided for
guests by their hotels.
After full-scale massage you can invariably feel every bone the
next day. There is, however, a more gentle treatment (ask for
"karuku kudasai" = softly please).
The charge for massage is generally about 5000 Yen. It is best
to ask in advance.

Motoring

Driving a car in Tokyo is an adventure in itself. There is
permanent traffic chaos on the narrow roads, and parking is a
complicated business. Accordingly visitors who are in the city
for only a short stay should be content to travel everywhere by
taxi or, in appropriate cases, by underground.
For those who despite this well-meant advice decide to be
bold, the following brief points should be made:

For the hire of a car (and with it permission to drive in Japan)
an International Driving Licence is required.

International Driving Licence

Vehicles travel on the left.

Driving on left

The speed limit on motorways is between 37 and 50 mph (60
and 80 km/h); the signs give the exact figure. On other roads
the limit is at times only $15\frac{1}{2}$ mph (25 km/h).

Speed limit

A hired car should never be left where there is a prohibition on
parking or waiting. In Tokyo 60,000 cars parked in contraven-
tion of the regulations are towed every day. Simply discovering
where the vehicle has been taken away to can occupy half a
day. The expense of recovering it is high, too.
The stores offer car-parking, but there is often little space.

Parking

See entry

Car hire

Museums

Tokyo is not a city which is visited for the sake of its art
collections. When a choice work of art finds its way here, as
happened when the Mona Lisa was loaned for exhibition,
visitors should be prepared to go out of their way to profit from
the opportunity. On that occasion millions were conveyed past
the picture at two-second intervals. Something similar still
happens in other places, especially on Sundays and public

Japanese Folkcraft Museum

Nezu Institute of Fine Arts

Okura-Shukokan Museum

holidays. Hordes of people are hurried on through the galleries by loudspeaker announcements. Accordingly, it is best to visit museums or art galleries on weekdays if possible.
Here is a selection:

Bridgestone Museum of Arts
Kyobashi-Chuo-ku (near Main Railway Station)
Railway: Main Railway Station
Underground: Nihombashi
Open: Daily (except Mon.) 10 a.m.–5 p.m.
It was founded by Ishibashi, the car tyre manufacturer; and the English translation of his name is "Bridgestone".
A collection of French Impressionists.

Communications Museum
See A-Z, Museum of Communications

Crafts Gallery
Underground: Takebashi
Open: Daily (except Mon.) 10 a.m.–5 p.m.
Japanese crafts are exhibited in this gallery. It is housed in a restored building from the Meiji Period and was opened in 1977.

Hatakeyama Collection
Underground: Takanawadai
Open: 1 April–15 June; 1 July–15 Sept.; 1 Oct.–15 Jan.; 8 Feb.–15 Mar. Daily (except Mon.) for all these dates, 10 a.m.–4.30 p.m.
Sumie pictures, works of art and craft objects connected with the tea ceremony. There are also temporary exhibitions.

Practical Information

Idemitsu Art Gallery
1–1, 3-chome, Marunouchi, Chiyoda-ku
Railway: Yurakucho
Open: Daily (except Mon.) 10 a.m.–5 p.m.
Works of art and craft objects from old Japan and neighbouring countries.

Japanese Sword Museum
See A–Z, Japanese Sword Museum

Japan Folkcraft Museum
Komaba Park
Railway: Komabo-Todaimae (Inokashira Line)
Open: Daily (except Mon.) 10 a.m.–5 p.m.
Exhibits from all parts of Japan and Korea; also examples of early and primitive art.

Meiji Treasure House
See A–Z, Meiji Shrine

Museum of Sumo
See A–Z, Sumo

National Museum of Modern Art
Kitanomaru Park, Chiyoda-ku
Underground: Takebashi
Open: Daily (except Mon.) 10 a.m.–5 p.m.
Contemporary 20th-c. Japanese art (Masao Tsuruoka, Toshinobu Onosato, Jiro Yoshihara, etc.).

National Museum of Tokyo
See A–Z, National Museum of Tokyo

National Museum of Western Art
See A–Z, National Museum of Western Art

National Science Museum
See A–Z, National Science Museum

Nezu Institute of Fine Art
Underground: Omotesando
Open: Daily (except Mon.) 9.30 a.m.–4.30 p.m.
More than 8000 ancient Oriental exhibits.

Okura-Shukokan Museum
Underground: Toranomon
Open: Daily (except Mon.) 10 a.m.–4 p.m.
Pictures, ceramics, swords, Buddhist art.

Paper Museum
See A–Z, Paper Museum

Pentax Gallery
Kasumicho Corp. 3–21-20 Nishi-Azabu, Minota-ku
Underground: Roppongi
Open: Daily (except Mon.) 10 a.m.–5 p.m.

Riccar Art Museum (Ukiyo-e-Museum)
2–3-6, Ginza, Chuo-ku
Underground: Ginza
Open: Daily (except Mon.) 11 a.m.–8 p.m.
Old Japanese wood engravings and handicrafts.

Science Museum
Kitanomaru Park
Underground: Takebashi
Open: Daily (except Mon.) 9.30 a.m.–4.30 p.m.
The exhibits illustrate progress from agriculture in the earliest times to present-day space research and the most modern products of Japanese technology.

Suntory Museum of Art
Palace Building, 1–1-1, Marunouchi, Chiyoda-ku
Railway: Main Railway Station
Underground: Akasaka-Mitsuke
Open: Daily (except Mon.) 10 a.m.–5 p.m.
Works of art and craft objects from the Feudal Period.

Takanawa Art Museum
4–10-30, Takanawa, Shiba, Minato-ku
Railway: Shinagawa
Open: Daily (except Mon.) 9 a.m.–4.30 p.m.
Works of art and craft objects from old Japan and China.

Tenri Museum
Tenrikyo-Kaikan Building, Mitoshire-cho
Railway: Kanda (Ginza Line)
Open: Daily 9 a.m.–5 p.m.
Folk and religious art.

Tokyo Metropolitan Art Gallery
See A–Z, Metropolitan Art Gallery of Tokyo

Tsubouchi Theatre Museum
See A–Z, Tsubouchi Theatre Museum

Yamatane Museum of Art
2–10, Kabuto-cho, Nihombashi, Chuo-ku
Underground: Kayabacho
Open: Daily (except Mon.) 11 a.m.–5 p.m.
Japanese painting from 1868 to the present day.

Music

Tokyo is a city where concerts are extremely popular. Foreign orchestras are always very popular when they come on visits, and the performances are invariably sold out. Performances by touring opera and ballet companies are also always extraordinarily well received.

Opera, Ballet, Concerts

The performances are given in the following halls:

Concert halls

NHK Hall
2–2-1, Jinnan, Shibuya-ku. Tel. 405–1111

Metropolitan Festival Hall
5–45, Ueno-Koen, Taito-ku. Tel. 828–2111

Hibiya Hall
1–3, Hibiya-Koen, Chiyoda-ku. Tel. 591–6388

Shibuya Hall
1–1, Udagawa-cho, Shibuya-ku. Tel. 463–5001

	Yamaha Hall 7–9-14, Ginza, Chuo-ku. Tel. 572–3111
Box offices	See entry

Newspapers

In English	The following appear daily in English: *Japan Times* *Asahi Evening News* *Mainichi Daily News* *The Daily Yomiuri* The following appear weekly in English: *Tokyo Weekender; Tour Companion.*
Foreign periodicals	Foreign periodicals are available in the hotel bookstalls and in many Western-style supermarkets.
Foreign newspapers	A good selection of quite recent foreign newspapers is available at Marunouchi Railway Station, South Exit.

Night-life

Tokyo's night-life is extremely lively and extremely expensive, but in many parts of the city it comes to an abrupt halt just before midnight. It is then that the bars close, and Japanese night owls make for home. Trains and underground carriages are crowded, and it is difficult to get a taxi. With 300,000 restaurants and countless bars no one needs particular recommendation. Visitors will probably concentrate on Akasaka, Ginza and Roppongi, parts of the city where Western customs are familiar.

Discos	Independent House, 6th Floor, Toa Kaikan, Kabukicho 12 Shinjuku-ku.
	Murgen, 8–17, Akasaka 3-chome, Minato-ku Crazy Horse, 18–12, Roppongi 3-chome, Minato-ku.
Cabarets/ Night-clubs	Crown, Ginza. Tel. 572–5511 Open: From 6 p.m. Closed: Sun. English-speaking hostesses.
	Club Charon, Social Akasaka Building (5th Floor) Akasaka. Tel. 586–4480 Open: From 7 p.m. Closed: Sun. Small night-club with English-speaking hostesses (fee). Piano music.
	Club Copacabana, Akasaka. Tel. 585–5811 Open: From 6 p.m. Closed: Sun. High-grade cabaret show. English-speaking hostesses (fee).
	Cordon Bleu, Akasaka. Tel. 582–7800 Open: from 7 p.m. Closed: Sun. Restaurant-Theatre. Topless dancers. French Cuisine.

Club Casanova, Roppongi. Tel. 584–4558
Open: From 6.30 p.m. Closed: Sun.
American shows, Rock 'n Roll music.

Cabaret Monte Carlo, Ginza. Tel. 571–6571
Open: From 6.30 p.m. Closed: Sun.
Variety show. English-speaking hostesses. (The fee for the
hostess, two drinks, show and cover charge are all included in
the entry charge.)

Club Morena, Roppongi. Tel. 402–9337
Open: From 7.30 p.m. Closed: Sun.
Three night-clubs in one building; Club Morena is the best
value.

People, Roppongi, Tel. 470–0555
Roppongi Square Building
Gay Club with transvestite shows. Before midnight there are
hostesses in the bar; after midnight this is a favoured meeting
place for homosexuals.
Open: From 6.30 p.m. Closed: Sun.

Ballantine, Kajimaya Building (2nd floor)   For music lovers
Roppongi (Jazz)

Birdland
Basement 2, Roppongi Square Building, Roppongi, Jazz

Gin-Paris, 9–11, Ginza 7-chome, French "chansons"

Taro, Kabuki-cho 21, Shinjuku-ku, Jazz

International Club 88, Unakami Building (3rd floor)   Strip clubs
3–11-6, Roppongi. Tel. 402–5436
Open: From 6 p.m. Closed: Sun.
Strip shows

L'Osier, Shiseido Parlor Building (7th floor)
Ginza. Tel. 572–2121
Open: From 6 p.m. Closed: Sun.
Italian-style ambiance.

Photography

Photographers can focus their cameras on practically everything in Japan without giving rise to offence. When Japanese
appear in really exotic costume it is, however, advisable, unless
it really is some crowded festival, to ask for permission to take
photographs by making a few appropriate gestures and saying
"sumisen" (i.e. "excuse me" or "would you mind?").
Permission is always readily granted. The Japanese themselves
take lots of photographs, especially of one another. It can often
happen that you find a camera being pressed into your hands
as a class of schoolgirls go by and you are asked to take a
photograph of the group. This always gives rise to general
hilarity.
Photographic equipment of every conceivable sort is available
in Japanese camera shops.

Group photograph in front of the Imperial Palace

Policeman in a Koban

Police

Tokyo – unlike New York, for instance – is a city where foreigners can move about without risk and go out on their own at any time of day or night. The number of crimes committed is decreasing here, unlike the experience of other large cities, and the detection rate is improving. Theft and crimes of violence are at the head of the crime figures.

A feature of Tokyo are the little cabins, called "kobans" at every major road junction. They are little observation posts for the police and are equipped with telephone, beds and cooking facilities. From them the officers maintain a watch all round the clock. It is from here, too, that they set out, generally in pairs, to patrol their beats. As they are for the most part posted to the same district for years on end they know every family and every address.

Kobans (Police boxes)

This arrangement is, moreover, very convenient for tourists. Visitors who have, for instance, lost their way should not hesitate to make for the nearest koban and ask for directions. If the policeman there cannot speak English he will phone the Central Police Station where there is always an interpreter on duty.

Pornography

In Japan the attitude to eroticism is traditionally broad-minded. What by Western standards would be considered pornographic is represented in much Japanese literature and art. It is also often encountered, and in unimaginably brutal forms in the adult "comics". Nonetheless, officials are very strict about the import of anything of a pornographic nature which might cause offence. Visitors should bear this in mind if they wish, for instance, to bring in, as a present perhaps, a volume of artistic reproductions of Rubens' paintings.

Hundreds of protectors of moral standards are said to be employed to blot out "objectionable material" in imported magazines with black felt-tips. Double standards in morality are universal.

Postal services

Tokyo Cho Yubinkyoku (Main Post Office) is open 24 hours a day.
The entry is near the Imperial Palace, the Dresdner Bank, Tokyo Eki, Marunouchi Exit.

Main Post Office

Post offices may be recognised by their symbol resembling a red T with two bars across the upright.
Because visitors may well have problems over language in the post offices and since the latter deal only with certain classes of business, it is best to go to the Main Post Office.

Post offices

Post offices are open Mon.–Fri. from 9 a.m. to 5 p.m., and Sat. from 9 a.m. to 12.30 p.m.

Opening times

Practical Information

Postal rates

Inland letters up to the standard weight of 25 g cost 50 Yen, and postcards 20 Yen.
Letters to Europe up to the standard weight of 10 g cost 140 Yen. On average, delivery to Europe takes four days. A letter weighing 20 g can be sent by surface mail for 90 Yen.

Stamps

Stamps may be obtained in hotels and post offices.

Post boxes

Post boxes are painted in different colours for different classes of mail. Red post boxes are for inland and foreign letters; blue ones for express mail.

Presents

When making a visit, the visitor offers some small gift, preferably something brought from Europe. It should not be too expensive because that can cause the host serious embarrassment, as it would then create an obligation of excessive regard. In Japan present-giving is something that has got quite out of hand. Visitors should resist the temptation. Twice a year is the correct interval. In the stores there are whole departents for the packing and despatch of gifts.

Programme of Events

Visiting companies

Advance information about cultural events such as concerts and performances of plays by visiting companies, may be obtained from:
International Musical Arts Service
2–21-2, Nishi-Azabu, Minato-ku. Tel. 400–3386.

Tokyo guides

In the hotels there are generally two city publicity "newspapers" available free – *Tour Companion* and *Weekender*. They contain information about all the events taking place in Tokyo. There are also shopping hints and generally precise instructions on how to find your way to shops.

Public holidays

The public holidays on which public offices are closed and most businessmen are unavailable are as follows:
1 January – New Year
15 January – Adults' Day
11 February – Celebration of foundation of the State
20 (21) March – first day of spring
29 April – the Emperor's birthday
1 May – Labour Day (In Tokyo there are big demonstrations setting out for Harajuku Railway Station; firms have to catch up on work afterwards.)
3 May – Constitution Day
5 May – Children's Day
15 September – Old People's Day
23 (24) September – First Day of Autumn
10 October – Sports' Day

3 November – Culture Day
23 November – Labour Thanksgiving Day
Should a national public holiday fall on a Sunday, the Monday
following is also a holiday.

Public transport

The fastest and cheapest means of public transport is by the
Underground Railways. Its network comprises ten lines. Trains
run from 5 a.m. until midnight.

The entrances to the Underground Stations are indicated by   Stations
distinctive signs – a wheel for a public line and a stylised S for
a private line. Large stations have various entrances which are
situated relatively far apart from one another.
Important. Sometimes an entrance gives access to just one line
which runs in a certain direction only. It is therefore essential to
discover in advance which line and, in some cases, which
direction you need.
The name of every station is displayed in Roman script as well
as in Japanese characters. Beneath the name two other names
are also given – that of the previous staion (on the right) and
that of the next station (on the left).

In the hotels, at travel agents (see entry) and at the Tourist   Underground
Information Offices (see entry) there are timetables with maps
of the individual lines printed in colour. Thus the Ginza line is
printed yellow, just as its coaches are all painted yellow, while
the Marunouchi line is red, like its coaches.
The important thing, when, for instance changing trains, in all
the stations, which are often underground, is to follow the
colour belonging to the line by which you want to travel.
Passengers will often be at a loss at a railway station for lack of
any knowledge of Japanese. But there is often a plan of the line
with English text and ticket prices displayed on the pillars.

Tickets cost a minimum of 80 Yen and go up in 20 Yen steps.   Fares
Tickets are obtained from automatic ticket issuing machines
which give change. If you cannot discover the correct fare,
either go to the ticket office or else buy a 100 Yen ticket from
one of the machines. When leaving the station you will then be
stopped by the ticket collector at the exit. You need only give
him the ticket and a few coins. There is no need to check your
change – the Japanese are very honest.

The Yamanote – with green painted coaches – stops at all major   Japan National Railways
stations.   (Kokuden)

The least expensive journeys cost 60 Yen. Passengers buy their   Fares
tickets from ticket machines and surrender them when leaving
the train. Passengers who cannot discover what the correct fare
is should buy any ticket and pay the excess on arrival.

Tokyo has a dense network of bus services. But even the   Buses
Foreign Travel Office admits in its handout that "though Tokyo
has a very extensive bus network, even locals find it confusing
to use. Visitors are accordingly better advised to travel by train
or underground."

Practical Information

Suggestion

Should a visitor discover himself stranded when making an outing by public transport and cannot find his way back for lack of any signs in Roman script or of any helpful Japanese who can give information in English, then he should hail the next taxi and show the driver the visiting card of his hotel. It is always a good idea to carry the latter.

Radio

Most of Japan's VHF stations cannot be heard on receivers built for European use, because the frequencies are quite different. The American military transmitter FEN on medium wave broadcasts news bulletins every hour on the hour.

Railway Stations

Main Railway Station
9–1 Marunouchi 1-chome, Chiyoda-ku.
The Daimaru store has been built into the Railway Station. In the station basement there are many shops and restaurants in long shopping streets which almost link up with Ginza. Visitors in need of information will find the Japan Travel Bureaus here most convenient. If need be, help is given in contacting somebody who can speak English.
The Shinkansen trains depart from here, as do also the trains for Kamakura.

Shinjuku Railway Station
38–1 Shinjuku 3-chome, Shinjuku-ku.
A store – Odakyu – has also been built on top of Shinjuku Station. This is the interchange station for the Chuo, Yamanote, and Seibu suburban lines. The Marunouchi Line runs out to Ikebukuro.

Ueno Railway Station
Chuo-dori, Taito-ku.
Departure point for the JNR lines to N Honshu.

Ikebukuro Railway Station
28 Ikebukuro 1-chome, Toshima-ku.
This is a changing point for suburban traffic on the lines which run out to the dormitory suburbs on the outskirts of Tokyo. There are also many restaurants and shops here.

Rail travel

The destination of any excursion which can conveniently be made from Tokyo is accessible by train. Travellers should enquire either in their hotel or at the Japan Travel Bureau (see Travel Agents) whether the trains depart from Shinjuku or Ueno Railway Stations.

Restaurants

Restaurant guides

Visitors who wish to forgo the European menus of their hotels and discover the gastronomic delights of Japanese cuisine (see Cuisine) should purchase in advance an English guide to Japanese cooking.

Display in a store restaurant

Eating cheap in Japan, published by Kimiko Nagasawa & Camy Condon is recommended.

This booklet contains precise instructions on how to recognise a Japanese restaurant by its appearance. It is above all of invaluable help because it has many coloured photographs which the visitor can show to the waiter. It also contains a list of the terms for all sorts of specialities, a few of the phrases needed for ordering and precise descriptions of dishes and eating habits.

Another equally valuable guide is called *122 Restaurants in Tokyo*. It is published by the Tokyo News Service. In it hungry visitors will find many international restaurants suggested, as well as Japanese ones.

There is a photograph of the exterior of every restaurant, and they are all marked on a plan. These can, of course, be shown to any taxi driver. The specialities of each restaurant are described, and details of prices are given. A small investment in these two booklets is well worthwhile.

The expression "Tourist Restaurants" may be a little mislead- | Tourist restaurants
ing. The restaurants listed below have been recommended by the Japanese Ministry for Tourists because they make arrangements for foreign guests and because English is generally spoken.

Akatombo
1–15-12, Toranomon,
Minato-ku. Tel. 501–0416.
Western cuisine.

Practical Information

Aoyama Diamond Hall
3–11-17, Kita-Aoyama,
Minatoku. Tel. 406–3261.
Japanese and Western cuisine.

Benihana Ikebukuro-ten
Air Castle Building,
1–1-25, Nishi Ikebukoto,
Toshima-ku. Tel. 985–6700.
Western cuisine.

Benihana of New York
6–3-7, Ginza,
Chuo-ku. Tel. 571–0700.
Speciality: Teppanyaki.

Brilliant
Shin Yurakucho Building,
1–12-1, Yurkucho,
Chiyoda-ku. Tel. 216–4261.
French cuisine.

Chinzanso
2–10-8, Sekiguchi,
Bunkyo-ku. Tel. 943–1111.
Japanese and Western cuisine.

Clark-Tei
Toho Seimei Building,
2–15-1, Shibuya, Shibuya-ku. Tel. 406–4188.
Speciality: Tonkatsu.

Furusato
3–4-1, Aobadei,
Meguro-ku. Tel. 463–2310.
Japanese cuisine.

Ginza Happo-en
6–4-7, Ginza,
Chuo-ku. Tel. 571–3432.
Japanese cuisine.

Ginza-yonchome Suehire
Kintetsu Building, 4–4-10, Ginza,
Chuo-ku. Tel. 562–0591.
Specialities: steak, Japanese style and Sukiyaki.

Happo-en
1–1-1, Shiroganedai,
Minato-ku. Tel. 443–3111.
Japanese cuisine.

Hasejin Azabu-ten
6–18, Iigura-katamachi, Azuba,
Minato-ku. Tel. 582–7811.
Speciality: Sukiyaki.

Hige-no-Tempi
1–6, Kyobashi,
Chuo-ku. Tel. 281–5585.
Speciality: Tempura.

Imaasa
Shimbashi-ekimae Building, 2–20-15, Shimbashi,
Minato-ku. Tel. 572–5286.
Speciality: Sukiyaki.

Inagiku, 2–6
Kayabacho, Nihombashi,
Chuo-ku. Tel. 669–5501.
Speciality: Tempura.

Isshin
1–13-8, Jingu-mae,
Shibuya-ku. Tel. 401–7991.
Japanese cuisine.

Jisaku
14–19, Akashicho, Tsukiii,
Chuo-ku. Tel. 541–2391.
Japanese cuisine.

Kakiden
Yasuyo Building (9th floor),
3–37, Shinjuku, Shinjuku-ku. Tel. 352–5121.
Speciality: Kaiseki.

Kanetanaka
7–18-17, Ginza,
Chuo-ku. Tel. 541–2556.
Japanese cuisine.

Kinsen
Kintetsu Building (5th floor),
4–4, Ginza,
Chuo-ku. Tel. 561–8708.
Japanese cuisine.

Kitcho
8–17-4, Ginza,
Chuo-ku. Tel. 541–8228.
Speciality: Kaiseki.

Kokeshiya
3–14-6, Nishi-Ogi-Minami,
Suginami-ku. Tel. 334–5111.
Western cuisine.

Kurawanka
Daian Building,
3–36-6, Shinjuku,
Shinjuku-ku. Tel. 352–5111.
Japanese cuisine.

Kikasa Maikan
5–5-17, Ginza,
Chuo-ku. Tel. 571–8181.
Japanese, Chinese and Western cuisine.

Mita
6–7, Nakasu, Hihombashi,
Chuo-ku. Tel. 666–5251.
Japanese cuisine.

Practical Information

New Tokyo Honten
2–4, Yurakucho,
Chiyoda-ku. Tel. 572–5711.
Japanese, Chinese and Western cuisine.

Restaurant Avion
2-3-1, Haneda-kuho,
Ota-ku. Tel. 747–0111.
Japanese, Chinese and Western cuisine.

Restaurant Isolde & Tristan
3–2-1, Nishi-azabu,
Minatoku. Tel. 478–1071.
French cuisine.

Restaurant Kinshabu
4–5-25, Ebisu,
Shibuya-ku. Tel. 442–6334.
Japanese cuisine.
Speciality: Shabu-shabu.

Restaurant Shiki Coq d'or
Toshiba Building,
5–2-1, Ginza,
Chuo-ku. Tel. 573–2121.
Western cuisine.

Restaurant Stockholm
Sweden Centre Building,
6–11-9, Roppongi,
Minato-ku. Tel. 403–9046.

Swedish Kitchen
Seryna,
3–12-2, Roppongi,
Minato-ku. Tel. 402–1051.
Japanese cuisine.

Shinjuka Gyuya
5–11-16, Shinjuku,
Shinjuku-ku. Tel. 352–2901.
Speciality: beef.

Suehiro
6–11-2, Ginza,
Chuo-ku. Tel. 571–9271.
Speciality: steaks.

Suehiro Asahi Edobashi-ten
3–13-11, Nihonbashi,
Chuo-ku. Tel. 271–8147.
Speciality: steaks.

Suchiro Asahi Tokyo-ten
6–11-2, Ginza
Chuo-ku. Tel. 573–0893.
Speciality: steaks.

Suehiro Asaha Yaesu
2–27-10, Hachobori,
Chuo-ku. Tel. 551–9158.
Speciality: steaks.

Suehiro Ginza Miyuki-ten
5–6-12, Ginza,
Chuo-ku. Tel. 573–5061.
Speciality: steaks.

Suehiro Kotobuki-ten
6–11-2, Ginza,
Chuo-ku. Tel. 571–0950.
Speciality: steaks.

Suehiro Jiyugaoka-ten
2–10-20, Jiyugaoka,
Meguro-ku. Tel. 723–2821.
Speciality: steaks.

Suehiro Sanno-ten
2–2-7, Omori-Sanno,
Ota-ku. Tel. 773–2718.
Speciality: steaks.

Suehiro Tsukiji-ten
4–1-15, Tsukiji,
Chuo-ku. Tel. 542–3951.
Speciality: steaks.

Ten-ichi
6–7-16, Ginza,
Chuo-ku. Tel. 571–1272.
Speciality: Tempura.

Totenko Ueno-ten
1–4-33, Ikenohata
Taito-ku. Tel. 828–5111.
Chinese cuisine.

Ueno Seiyoken
4–58 Ueno Park,
Taito-ku. Tel. 821–2181.
Western cuisine.

Yaesu-Chinzanso
1–8-3, Marunouchi,
Chiyoda-ku. Tel. 215–2131.
Japanese and Western cuisine.

YMCA Restaurant
7, Mitoshirocho, Kanda,
Chiyoda-ku. Tel. 292–7241.
Western cuisine.

Kosugi Kaikan Hachioji-ten
6–7, Yokamachi,
Hachioji City. Tel. (0426) 23–2111.
Japanese and Western cuisine.

In the stores (see entry) very good meals are available. The restaurants are generally open between 11 a.m. and 9 p.m. They are situated either on the top floor or in the two basements. There are no insurmountable problems over getting what you want.

Practical Information

You select what you want to eat from what is on display in the glass showcases by the entrance. After noting the numbers (or, better still, jotting them down) you go up to the cash desk, show or state the numbers and pay your bill. After that you select a seat at a table and wait for a waiter or waitress to whom you hand the ticket you have been given at the cash desk. The dishes you have selected are then brought to you at your table.

Restaurants in shopping centres

The gigantic shopping centres under the railway stations and in the underground stations all have restaurants, too. They are open daily from 11 a.m. to 9 p.m.

Coffee Houses

These are not at all the equivalent of European cafés, though coffee is served in them. The speciality is generally live musical performances. Some go in for pop, others for classical music or jazz and so on.

Ryokan

Japanese inns are called Ryokan (see A–Z, Ryokan). Visitors who feel inclined to spend a night in one of these Ryokans should inform themselves about the customs observed in Ryokans and do their best to surmount the language barrier. Here is a selection of addresses in Tokyo:
Fukudaya
6, Kioicho, Chiyodaku. Tel. 261–8577.
Shinkomatsu
1–9-13 Tsukiji, Chuo-ku. Tel. 541–2225.
Hotel Yaesu Ryumeikan
1–3-22, Yaesu. Chuo-ku. Tel. 271–0971.
Kegon
1–39-8, Yoyogi, Shubijy-ku. Tel. 370–3333.
Kin-eikaku
2–26, Toyotama-kami, Nerimaku. Tel. 991–1186.

Information

Information and advice about Ryokans in Tokyo and in Japan in general can be obtained from the Japanese information bureaus (see Information).

Shopping Centres

Akihabara

See A–Z, Akihabara

Ameya-Yokocho Lane

District: Taito-ku
Railway station: Okachimachi or Ueno (Keihin-Tohoku Line; Yamanote Line)
This market street, one of the liveliest in Tokyo, lies between Ueno Station and Okachimachi Station. On sale are food, sports and imported goods, clothes and leather goods.

Ginza

See A–Z

Harajuka

District: Shibuya-ku
Railway Station: Harajuku (Yamanote Line)
Underground Station: Meiji-Jingu-Mae (Chiyoda Line)
Jeans, leather goods, accessories, Parisian haute couture.

Ikebukuro

See A–Z

See A–Z   Kanda

See A–Z   Shinjuku

Shopping hours

Stores are generally open from 10 a.m. to 6 p.m. every day   Stores
including Sundays. But on certain weekends they are,
however, closed (see Stores). It is best to check in one of the
English-language newspapers.
The small Japanese shops open about 10 a.m. and close at
10 p.m. They, too, are open on Sundays.

See entry   Banks

See entry   Chemists

Sightseeing

The hotels have available a great number of leaflets about   Circular tours by bus
sightseeing tours around Tokyo by bus. Further information
may also be obtained from the Travel Agents (see entry) who
arrange these trips.
There are morning, afternoon and whole-day tours which
provide opportunities of seeing Tokyo's major sights. Some of
them include Kimono and Ikebana displays in their programmes, and also visits to studios where woodcuts are
printed.

The Seven Wonders of Tokyo   Special tours
This is a whole-day tour including a visit to the Arts and Crafts
Museum, Jomyoin Temple and a costume display.
Operator: Japan Travel Bureau

Art Around Tour
This is a whole-day tour including a visit to an Ikebana and to
a Kimono School as well as to a doll factory and to a gallery
specialising in coloured woodcuts.
Operator: Japan Travel Bureau

Village Life and Crafts
A whole-day tour, including displays of paper-folding, Bonsai
culture and doll-making.
Operator: Japan Travel Bureau

Tokyo by Night
Evening tours generally include a Japanese meal, a Kabuki
show (see A–Z, Kabuki) a visit to a night-club and a Geisha
party.
Operator: Japan Travel Bureau, Japan Grey Line.

City tours can either be booked at the visitor's hotel or by   Operators
telephone call to the following operators:
Japan Travel Bureau. Tel. 274–3921.
Fujita Travel Service. Tel. 573–1011.
Japan Grey Line. Tel. 436–6881.
As the special tours do not run every day, it is necessary to ask
for information in advance.

Practical Information

Cultural Events	See entry

Visit to a Japanese family

An organised visit to a Japanese family should make it possible for a foreigner to gain a deeper understanding of Japanese family life. These visits normally last one or two hours and are free apart from some small expenditure for some little gift (see Presents). They take place with families who have freely offered to receive foreign visitors.

Any expenses for transport and interpreting are paid for by the visitor.

Visits of this sort should be booked at least one day in advance. For information, consult the JNTO Tourist Information Centre (see Tourist information).

Visits to industry

It is not only tea, temples and Samurai that have made Japan world-famous. For most visitors from abroad Japan is a modern industrialised nation whose TV sets, cars, cameras and pocket calculators are sold in five continents. It is possible, moreover, for visitors to see how these miracles of ingenious technology are manufactured. The Japan Travel Bureau organises day-long tours of various firms, including, for instance, Sony, Canon Cameras and Asahi Brewery. A tour takes place every week on Tuesday and Friday, and includes a midday meal and a chance to talk with the managers.

Travel Boutique

Since the end of 1980 there has been a new way of exploring the maze of streets that make up Tokyo in a pleasant and instructive fashion. Masaka Osodo, a Tokyo housewife, had the idea of offering a new service to tourists from abroad. In the Shinjuku district of the city – near the S exit from the station – she opened Travel Boutique 747. There a dozen girl students with an excellent command of English are always available for city tours. A day, using only public transport, costs upwards of 5000 Yen, or else taxis can be taken for an additional fee.

Visitors can say what they would like to see, or else they can ask the girls to take charge entirely, which often means there is a chance to get to know either a specialised restaurant or a snack bar and learn about local eating habits. The groups are deliberately kept small. Tours take place on Saturdays. Special arrangements are, however, possible (tel. 310–9041).

Japan Guide Association

Another possibility for individual guided tours is by the Japan Guide Association, tel. 213–2706. It also arranges interpreters (see entry). Groups can be up to four persons, and the charges are from about 15,000 Yen per day in English (or higher for other languages).

Sitting

It is only in comparatively recent times that chairs were introduced into Japan. In Ryokans, at home and in restaurants people still sit on the floor on many occasions; the typical sitting position generally stops the flow of blood in Westerners' limbs. After they have ventured out to visit a restaurant foreigners (Gaijin) are frequently to be seen hobbling along the streets of Tokyo. They have to keep their limbs moving for a long time before they can walk normally. The little cushions that are spread out for guests are really no help at all.

Sitting is something that has to be learnt

Souvenirs

A shopping expedition normally starts at Ginza, where practically all the large stores (see entry) are to be found. Here at least somebody can usually be found who speaks English and can help over purchases. It is best to look out for Kimonos, fabrics, magnificent printed paper and also, of course, for pearls, pottery and ebony carvings, for which Japan is famous.

Kimonos, fabrics and pearls

Also recommended are wood-block prints which are still being printed from the original blocks made by the country's great masters. The quality is excellent, and the prices reasonable, from about 5000 Yen upwards. As the stores also function as galleries (see entry) and have regular exhibitions, the service there is first-class. Before embarking on a shopping expedition it is worth checking in an English-language newspaper which stores are closed. They are all open at the weekend, but they are not all open every day.

Wood-block prints

See A–Z, Kanda

Books

Visitors looking for transistors, loudspeakers or any other entertainment products from Japan's famous electronics industry should go to Akihabara (see A–Z).

Electronics

Whether seeking cosmetics or TV sets, cameras or watches, visitors can save up to 15% on the normal sale price by going to one of the so called "tax-free shops". They can be found in

Tax-free shops

141

Souvenirs

hotels as well as in the most popular shopping districts such as Ginza, Shibuya or Shinjuku. A passport is required. To it the salesman staples a "record of purchase" which he has filled in. When the visitor leaves Japan that is taken as evidence that the objects which have been bought have not been used in Japan itself.

Specialist shops

English literature	Kinokuniya Near Main Railway Station, Shinju-ku. Open: Mon.–Sun. 10 a.m.–7 p.m. Closed: 1st and 3rd Wed. of month. Jena Near Ginza Underground Station. Open: Mon–Sat. 10.30 a.m.–7.50 p.m.; Sun. 12.30–6.45 p.m. Closed: holidays.
Maps, newspapers	In all large stores
Fabrics	Fashion World Toa 23–6, Udagawa-cho Shibuya-ku. Tel. 463–3311.
Silks	Kawamura-Silk 8–9-17, Ginza, Chuo-ku. Tel. 572–0181.

Washington Shoe Store   Shoes
Ginza.
Men's shoes.

Isetan Department Store   Ladies' clothes
Shinjuku ("Queens Corner").
In the hosiery department there are tights up to size 3.

Hanae Mor Boutique
Arcade of Hotel Imperial and Okura.
The firm makes clothes for export, so large sizes available.
Smart and expensive.

In the big stores (see entry)   Kimonos

See entry   Antiques

See Galleries; See Stores   Art

Sport

Visitors keen on Judo (see A–Z) can watch training and   Judo
displays from the spectators' galleries at:

Kodokan Judo Hall
Rail: Kasuga
Underground: Korakuen (Marunouchi Line).
Open: Daily (except Sun. and holidays) 4–7.30 p.m.
Entry free.

Nippon Budokan Hall
Rail: Kudanshita.
Underground: Kudanshita.
Open: Daily (except Sun. and holidays) 5–8 p.m.
Entry free.

This, too, may be viewed from the spectators' galleries.   Kendo
Nippon Budokan Hall
Underground: Kudanshita.
Open: Daily (except Sun. and holidays) 5–8 p.m.
Entry free.

Karate training may be watched from the spectators' galleries   Karate
at:
Japan Karate Association (Nippon Karate Gyogai).
Tel. 462–1415.
Rail Ebisu.
Open: Daily (except Sun. and holidays) 10.30–11.30 a.m.;
4–5 p.m. and 6–7 p.m.
Entry free.

Spectators and observers are also allowed in to watch Aikido.   Aikido
Aikido World Headquarters
Rail: Shinjuku (thence by taxi).
Open : Sun. 9–10 and 10.30–11.30 a.m.; Mon.–Sat. 6.30–7.30,
8–9 a.m.; 3–4, 5.30–6.30 and 7–8 p.m.

Kendo – a "sword fight" with wooden batons

Sumo wrestlers

There are Sumo tournaments, which last fifteen days, and are held three times a year in Tokyo – in January, May and September (see A–Z, Sumo). The events take place at Kuramae Kogugikan.

Horse racing was imported from abroad, but the Japanese passion for betting has made the sport popular throughout the land. The most important meetings are at Fuchu, at the Tokyo Race Course – 20 miles (35 km) W – and at Samezumachi, at Oi Race Course – 8 miles (12 km) S of Tokyo.
Betting is under state control and offers poor odds. In particular the system is so complicated that it is virtually impossible for foreigners to participate.

Stores

Tokyo's stores are well worth visiting. The impression is overwhelming, such is the range of goods on offer and the quality of the service. The staff are familiar with dealing with visitors from abroad. English is understood and spoken, so there is usually no language problem for shoppers.
From souvenirs (see entry) to ancient works of art (see Antiques), everything can be found under one roof. Shoppers can have a meal in the store, sit and rest awhile and look round an art exhibition.
As well as objects particular to the Japanese lifestyle, Western consumer goods can also be purchased.
There are many stores in the Shinjuku district and in Ginza. Visitors going for a stroll around Ginza can combine this with a shopping expedition to a department store.
The stores are always open at weekends, but closed one day each week. In case of doubt, consult any English-language newspaper – or the hotel porter.

Mitsukoshi. Tel. 562–1111.
Closed: Mon.

Hankyu. Tel. 573–2231.
Closed: Thurs.

Matsuya. Tel. 567–1211.
Closed: Thurs.

Matsuzakaya. Tel. 572–1111.
Closed: Wed.

Mitsukoshi. Tel. 354–1111.
Closed: Mon.

Isetan. Tel. 352–1111.
Closed: Wed.

Keio. Tel. 342–2111.
Closed: Thurs.

Odakyu. Tel. 342–1111.
Closed: Thurs.

Practical Information

Other stores

Mitsukoshi, Nihonbashi. Tel. 241–3311.
Closed: Mon.

Daimaru, Tokyo Station Building. Tel. 212–8011.
Closed: Wed.

Takashimaya, Nihonbashi. Tel. 211–4111.
Closed: Wed.

Tokyu, Nihonbashi. Tel. 211–0511.
Closed: Thurs.

Tokyu, Shibuya Station Building. Tel. 477–3111.
Closed: Thurs.

Swimming Pools

Swimming pools in hotels

Also open to non-residents (a selection):

New Otani. Tel. 265–1111 (garden pool).
Open: end of June–early Sept.

Akasaka Prince. Tel. 262–5151.
Open: 1 June–15 Sept.

Tokyo Prince. Tel. 434–4221.
Open: 1 June–15 Sept.

Hotel Takanawa. Tel. 443–9251.
Open: 1 July–31 Aug.

Geihinkan Shirogane Prince. Tel. 444–1231.
Open: 1 June–15 Sept.

Haneda Tokyu. Tel. 747–0311 (Haneda Airport).
Open: mid June–mid Sept.

Open-air pools

Tokyo Marine. Tel. 896–3111.
Rail: Tobuisezaki Line.
Open: mid June–mid Sept.

Shinagawa Sportsland. Tel. 442–7171.
Rail: Shinagawa.
Open: end May–end Aug.

Meiji Jingu Pool. Tel. 403–3456.
Rail: Sendagaya.
Open: early June–mid Sept.

Korukuen Pool. Tel. 811–2111.
Rail: Suidobashi.
Open: 31 May–31 Aug.

Tokyo Kosei Nenkin Sports Centre Pool. Tel. 415–2080.
Rail: Odakyu-Line, Seijogakuenmae.
Open: 1 July–mid Sept.

Nipponkaku Rainbow Pool. Tel. 367–2222.
Rail: Higaschinakano.
Open: 1 June–early Sept.

Shibura Sport Centre Jumbo Pool. Tel. 969–9211
Shimura 3-chome, Tokyo.
Rail: Metropolitan.
Open: mid June–early Sept.

Toshimaen Pool. Tel. 990–3131.
Rail: Seibu-Line, Toshimaen.
Open: 1 June–mid Sept.

Yoyogi Stadium Pool. Tel. 468–1171 (heated).
Rail: Harajuku.
Open: throughout year.

Tokyo Taiikukan Indoor Pool. Tel. 408–6191.
Rail: Sendagaya.
Open: throughout year.

Public indoor swimming pools

Taxis

In Tokyo there are adequate numbers of taxis, and using them is reasonably economical. They wait outside the stations and hotels. A moving taxi can be hailed simply by waving at it. Most taxi-drivers do not know much English, so it is important not only to have the address written down but also to show them your destination on a map. They do not expect to be offered a tip.

Taxi doors open and shut automatically.

Public transport ceases to operate about midnight. At that time it is difficult to get a taxi. In Ginza and throughout the city there are long queues everywhere. It is best to go to a taxi rank as waving down taxis is futile at this time of night.

When a taxi is going past, you can tell from the green light behind the windscreen whether it is for hire and by the red light that it is already hired. If they stop even when the green light is showing, you have to hold up two fingers to indicate that you are prepared to pay double fare. At night the taximeters go round faster because the rates are higher.

It is not usual to hire taxis by phone, but it is possible. Here are some numbers:

Taxi hire by telephone

Daiwa, Otemachi. Tel. 201–7007.
Eastern Motors, Nishi-Shimbashi. Tel. 503–0171.
Fuji, Ginza. Tel. 551–6411.
Green Cab, Setagaya. Tel. 417–2221.
Hato Bus. Tel. 231–0566.
Hinomaru, Akasaka. Tel. 583–8146.
Nihon, Otemachi. Tel. 231–4871.
Seibu, Shiba Park. Tel. 432–7581.
Taiyo, Tsukuji. Tel. 541–2141.
Takara, Roppongi. Tel. 403–7931.
Teito, Otemachi. Tel. 214–2021.

Tea ceremony

See A–Z, Tea Ceremony, and also see Cultural Events

Telegrams

Telegrams in Roman script are accepted everywhere, in telegraph offices, post offices and railway stations.

Telephones

There are various types of telephones which are distinguished by colour.

Telephone kiosks | Public telephone kiosks are blue (or very occasionally red).

Small red telephones | Small red telephones are for local calls only. The coin boxes take only one 10 Yen coin at a time, and the length of call allowed for that is 3 minutes. Just before the end of that period a warning tone sounds. The caller can then put in another coin, or the call ends automatically.

Large red telephones | Large red telephones are for long-distance as well as local calls. they take up to six 10 Yen coins.

Blue telephones | These, too, are for both long-distance and local calls, but accept more coins, up to a maximum of ten 10 Yen coins.

Yellow telephones | These can be used for local calls, but are mainly intended for long-distance inland calls. Accordingly they accept a larger amount of money, up to ten 10 Yen and nine 100 Yen coins.

Note | Money should be put in before the number is dialled. As soon as a warning tone is heard, more money must be put in or the call will be interrupted. Any unused coins are returned.

Overseas calls | For information in English call 0051. The cost of a one-minute call to Europe is 3230 Yen.

Theatres

For the traditional Japanese theatrical forms of Noh, Bunraku and Kabuki, see the entries under A–Z.
The addresses of theatres where these performances may be seen are:

Noh | Ginza Noh-Theatre (Ginza Nohakudo Hall)
5–15, Ginza 6-chome, Chuo-ku. Tel. 571-0197.
Railway: Ginza.

Kanze Noh Theatre (Kanze Nohgakudo Hall)
16–4, Shoto 1-chome, Shibuya-ku. Tel. 469–5241.
Railway: Shibuya.

Kita Noh Theatre (Kita Nohgakudo Hall)
6–9, Kami-Osaki 4-chome, Shinagawa-ku. Tel. 491–7773.
Railway: Meguro.

National Theatre
13, Hayabusacho, Chiyoda-ku. Tel. 265–7411.
Underground: Nagatacho.

See A–Z, Bunraku.   Bunraku

National Theatre   Kabuki
See above

Kabukiza Theatre
4–3, Ginza-Higashi, Chuo-ku. Tel. 541–3131.
Underground: Higashi-Ginza.

See entry   Cultural Events

See entry   Box offices

Times for Visits

Public offices are generally open on weekdays between 9 a.m.   Public offices
and noon and 1 p.m. and 5 p.m., and on Sat. from 9 a.m. to
noon.

Business visits are usually made between 10 a.m. and noon and   Business visits
from 2.30 p.m. to 5 p.m.

Tipping

In Japan there is no need for percentage calculations. Tips are
not generally accepted, because the customer, whether in a
shop or a restaurant, has already paid for his order. The
exceptions are the Western-style hotels, where the liftboys
expect about 200 Yen for taking a suitcase up to a room, and
taxi-drivers who have had to deal with a lot of luggage.

Toilets

In this matter visitors must generally adapt to local ways. What
visitors find is frequently not the opportunity of sitting at ease
but rather a basin set in the floor and slightly protruding. This
means that going to the lavatory is not always particularly
comfortable, but in the subtropical climate of Japan there are
no doubt advantages as regards hygiene. Visitors from the S
parts of Europe will not find Japanese toilet arrangements
entirely unfamiliar.
Visitors needing the toilet should ask the waiter the way to
"ote-arai", "to-ire" and, if that produces no response, "benjo".
Out in the street there are no "benjos". One has to call at the
next hotel or café.

Tourist Information

As a consequence of language difficulties visitors generally   In Tokyo
have to ask advice from their hotels or from some good friends.
If there are any problems over visas, the following can be of
assistance:

Practical Information

Tokyo Immigration Office
3–20, Konan 3-chome, Minato-ku.
Tel. 471–5111.

Japan National Tourist Organisation (JNTO)
10–1, Yurakucho 2-chome, Chiyoda-ku,
J-100 Tokyo.
Tel. (03) 502 1461.

In Great Britain

167 Regent Street
London W1.
Tel. (01) 734 9638.

In U.S.A.

Rockefeller Plaza
630 Fifth Avenue,
New York. NY 10111.
Tel. (212) 757 5640.

For general information, booking of sightseeing tours and excursions, visitors should contact the following:

Tourist Information Centres (Information Bureaus in the city and at Narita Airport).

Tokyo Office
Kotani Building,
6–6, Yurakucho 1-chome,
Chiyoda-ku. Tel. 502–1461.
Open: Mon.–Fri. 9 a.m.–5 p.m.; Sat. 9 a.m.–1 p.m.
Closed: Sun., holidays.

New Tokyo Airport Office (Narita Airport)
Airport Terminal Building,
Narita, Chiba Prefecture. Tel. (0476) 32–8711.
Open: Mon.–Fri. 9 a.m.–8 p.m.; Sat. 9 a.m.–noon.
Closed: Sun., holidays.

Japan Travel Bureau
Foreign Tourist Department
1–13-1 Nihonbashi,
Chuo-ku. Tel. 276–7803.

Travel Agents

See entry

Teletourist service

Information about current events:
In English. Tel. 503–2911.
In French. Tel. 503–2926.

Travel Agents

Everett Travel Service
Kokusai Building,
3–12 Marunouchi,
Chiyoda-ku. Tel. 201–4171.

Fujita Travel Service
Godo Building,
6–6 Ginza Nishi,
Chuo-ku. Tel. 573–1011.

Japan Grey Line
Pelican Building,
3–3-3, Nishi Shinbashi, Minato-ku. Tel. 433–4801.

Japan Travel Bureau
1–6-4 Marunouchi,
Chiyoda-ku. Tel. 274–3921.

Travel documents

Visitors from the United Kingdom entering Japan need only a
valid passport, provided their stay in the country does not
exceed six months.
For a stay in Japan of up to 12 months a visa, provided free,
must be obtained. The grant of a visa does not, however,
constitute a work permit. The latter will only be granted after a
complicated procedure has been gone through according to
trade or profession and after certified declarations from the
home country have been deposited.

Smallpox and cholera inoculation certificates are required only
from visitors from countries where these diseases are endemic.
Information about which regions fall under this regulation at
any particular time will be provided by the Japanese Foreign
Travel Agency (see Tourist Information), and travel agents. The
Japanese embassies and consulates in the United Kingdom,
etc. may also be consulted.

Inoculation certificates

Vaccination and inoculation centres

For Japan itself there is generally no need for inoculations (see
Travel Documents). But visitors who decide while they are in
Tokyo to go on to some other country where inoculations are
obligatory, should note the following addresses:

Hibiya Clinic (English)
Hibiya Mitsui Building (1st floor). Tel. 502–2681.
Consultations: Mon–Fri. 9.30 a.m.–noon;
1–4.45 p.m.; Sat. mornings only.

Ken Eki Jo
3–9-35, Kohnan, Minato-ku. Tel. 471–7922.
Consultations: Mon, Wed., Thurs., Fri. 10–11.30 a.m.;
1.30– 4 p.m.

Miyairi Clinic
Kotsu Kaikan Building (2nd floor), near Yurakucho, Station,
Yurakucho Chiyoda-ku. Tel. 214–1511.
Consultations: Mon–Fri. 9.30 a.m.–noon; 1–4 p.m.; Sat.
mornings only.

Visiting cards (Meishi)

In Japan visiting cards are a necessity of life.
Introductions begin with an exchange of visiting cards.
Accordingly it is not only businessmen who should provide
themselves with an appropriately large number of these cards

but also any other visitors who expect to come into contact with Japanese.

There are firms in Tokyo which print visiting cards in the appropriate foreign language and in Japanese in a few hours:

Iwahagana Printing Inc.
3–16, Meijidori, Nishiodubo, Shinjuku-ku. Tel. 209–3381.

Wakabayashi Name Card Printing Factory
1–25, Sudacho, Kanda, Chiyoda-ku. Tel. 255–7909.

Voltage

Most electrical appliances cannot be used here, even if provided with a transformer. The electricity supply in Tokyo is 100 volts.

Weights and Measures

In this connection British visitors should not have too much difficulty as in Japan the metric system applies.

Youth Hostels

Ichigaya Youth Hostel
1–6, Gobancho, Chiyoda-ku. Tel. 261–6839.
Tokyo 102.
128 beds.

Yoyogi Youth Hostel
No. 14 OMYC, 3–1, Kamizono-cho. Tel. 467–9163.
Yoyogi, Shibuya-ku. Tokyo 151.
150 beds.

Asia Centre of Japan
8–10-32 Akasaka, Minato-ku. Tel. 402–6111.
178 beds.

Japan YWCA.
4–8-8 Kudan Minami, Chiyoda-ku. Tel. 264–0661.
9 rooms: women only.

Shin Nakano Lodge
6–1-1 Honmachi, Nakano-ku. Tel. 381–4886.
9 rooms.

Tokyo YMCA
7, Mitoshiro-cho, Kanda, Chiyoda-ku. Tel. 293–1911.
100 rooms: men only.

Tokyo YWCA
1–8, Kanda Surugadai, Chiyoda-ku. Tel. 293–5421.
25 rooms: women only.

Tokyo YWCA Sadahara
3–1-1 Ichigaya, Sadohara-cho, Shinyuku-ku. Tel. 268–7313.
24 rooms: for women and married couples only.

Useful Telephone Numbers at a Glance

Emergency Services
    Ambulance   119
    Fire Brigade   119
    Police   110

Information
    Flight Reservations (Narita Airport)   665–7135
    Narita Airport   (0476) 32–8711
    Flight Information   665–7156
    Events (Teletourist) in English   503–2911
                   in French   503–2926

Diplomatic Representatives
    United Kingdom   (03) 265 5511
    United States   (03) 583 7141
    Canada   (03) 408 2101

Airline Companies
    Japan Air Lines   747–1111

Lost Property Offices
    Buses   216–2953
    Private Railways   216–2953
    Japan National Railways (Main Station)   231–1880
    City Police HQ   478–1547
    Taxi Central Office   355–0300
    Underground Railways (Ueno Station)   834–5577

Travel Agents
    Everett Travel Service   201–4171
    Fujita Travel Service   573–1011
    Japan Grey Line   433–4801
    Japan Travel Bureau   274–3921

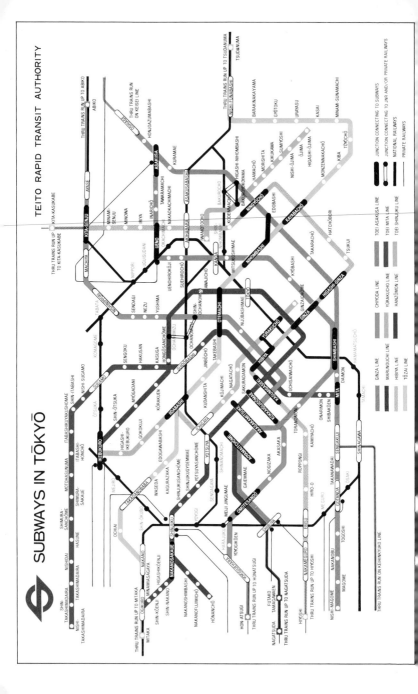

Notes

Notes

Notes

Baedeker's Travel Guides

"The maps and illustrations are lavish. The arrangement of information (alphabetically by city) makes it easy to use the book."

—San Francisco Examiner-Chronicle

What's there to do and see in foreign countries? Travelers who rely on Baedeker, one of the oldest names in travel literature, will miss nothing. Baedeker's bright red, internationally recognized covers open up to reveal fascinating A-Z directories of cities, towns, and regions, complete with their sights, museums, monuments, cathedrals, castles, gardens and ancestral homes—an approach that gives the traveler a quick and easy way to plan a vacation itinerary.

And Baedekers are filled with over 200 full-color photos and detailed maps, including a full-size, fold-out roadmap for easy vacation driving. Baedeker—the premier name in travel for over 140 years.

Please send me the books checked below and fill in order form on reverse side.

☐ **Austria**	$14.95	☐ **Mediterranean Islands**	$14.95
0-13-056127-4		0-13-056862-7	
☐ **Caribbean**	$14.95	☐ **Mexico**	$14.95
0-13-056143-6		0-13-056069-3	
☐ **Egypt**	$15.95	☐ **Netherlands, Belgium, and**	
0-13-056358-7		**Luxembourg**	$14.95
☐ **France**	$14.95	0-13-056028-6	
0-13-055814-1		☐ **Portugal**	$14.95
☐ **Germany**	$14.95	0-13-056135-5	
0-13-055830-3.		☐ **Provence/Cote d'Azur**	$9.95
☐ **Great Britain**	$14.95	0-13-056938-0	
0-13-055855-9		☐ **Rhine**	$9.95
☐ **Greece**	$14.95	0-13-056466-4	
0-13-056002-2		☐ **Scandinavia**	$14.95
☐ **Israel**	$14.95	0-13-056085-5	
0-13-056176-2		☐ **Spain**	$14.95
☐ **Italy**	$14.95	0-13-055913-X	
0-13-055897-4		☐ **Switzerland**	$14.95
☐ **Japan**	$15.95	0-13-056044-8	
0-13-056382-X		☐ **Tuscany**	$9.95
☐ **Loire**	$9.95	0-13-056482-6	
0-13-056375-7		☐ **Yugoslavia**	$14.95
		0-13-056184-3	

Please turn the page for an order form and a list of additional Baedeker Guides.

A series of city guides filled with colour photographs and detailed maps and floor plans from one of the oldest names in travel publishing:

Please send me the books checked below:

☐ **Amsterdam** $10.95
　0-13-057969-6
☐ **Athens**. $10.95
　0-13-057977-7
☐ **Bangkok** $10.95
　0-13-057985-8
☐ **Berlin** $10.95
　0-13-367996-9
☐ **Brussels** $10.95
　0-13-368788-0
☐ **Copenhagen**. $10.95
　0-13-057993-9
☐ **Florence** $10.95
　0-13-369505-0
☐ **Frankfurt**. $10.95
　0-13-369570-0
☐ **Hamburg** $10.95
　0-13-369687-1
☐ **Hong Kong** $10.95
　0-13-058009-0
☐ **Jerusalem** $10.95
　0-13-058017-1
☐ **London** $10.95
　0-13-058025-2

☐ **Madrid** $10.95
　0-13-058033-3
☐ **Moscow** $10.95
　0-13-058041-4
☐ **Munich** $10.95
　0-13-370370-3
☐ **New York** $10.95
　0-13-058058-9
☐ **Paris** $10.95
　0-13-058066-X
☐ **Rome** $10.95
　0-13-058074-0
☐ **San Francisco** $10.95
　0-13-058082-1
☐ **Singapore** $10.95
　0-13-058090-2
☐ **Tokyo** $10.95
　0-13-058108-9
☐ **Venice**. $10.95
　0-13-058116-X
☐ **Vienna**. $10.95
　0-13-371303-2

PRENTICE HALL PRESS

Order Department—Travel Books
200 Old Tappan Road
Old Tappan, New Jersey 07675

In U.S. include $1 postage and handling for 1st book, 25¢ each additional book. Outside U.S. $2 and 50¢ respectively.

Enclosed is my check or money order for $_____

NAME_____

ADDRESS_____

CITY_____STATE_____ZIP_____